Design Education

The proceedings of the Design Education section of an international conference on design policy held at the Royal College of Art, London, 20–23 July 1982

A conference organised by the Department of Design Research at the Royal College of Art in collaboration with the Design Research Society and The Design Council

Edited by
Richard Langdon, Department of Design Research, RCA
Ken Baynes, Department of Design Education, RCA
Phil Roberts, Department of Design Education, RCA

Design Policy: Design Education

Published in the United Kingdom in 1984 by
The Design Council
28 Haymarket
London SW1Y 4SU

Designed by Jane Starrett

Printed and bound in the United Kingdom by
Whitefriars Press, Tonbridge

© 1984
Ken Baynes, Phil Roberts, Arturo F.Montagu,
Anthony K.Russell, Nathan H.Shapira, A.E.Churches,
G.H.A.van Eyk, Avram Grant, Roger A.Gale, R.C.Sale,
Eileen Adams, Herman Neuckermans, Dietmar Palloks

British Library CIP Data

Design policy.
  Vol. 5: Design education
  1. Design
  I. Langdon, Richard
  745.4   NK1510

  ISBN 0-85072-147-4
  ISBN 0-85072-142-3 (set)

Editor's preface

Richard Langdon

The international conference on design policy held in London in 1982 can be seen as part of a series which started with a meeting of those concerned with design methods in London in 1962, and resulted in the formation of the Design Research Society. The Design Research Society has since then organised a number of conferences and symposia:

The Design Method Birmingham 1965
Design Methods in Architecture Portsmouth 1967
Design Participation Manchester 1971
Design and Behaviour Birmingham 1972
Problem Identification for Design Manchester 1974
Changing Design Portsmouth 1976
Design Science Method Portsmouth 1980

There have also been a number of conferences relating to the theme of design policy. The first, *Design Policy in Industry*, was organised by the then Council of Industrial Design and was held at the Royal College of Art in 1951; it was followed in 1956 by a second conference on *The Management of Design*. A conference which dealt with the wider social and political issues was held at the University of Princeton in 1964, the proceedings being published under the title *Who Designs America?* [1]

It was from the *Design Science Method* conference that a proposal for a further conference was made which would focus on social and political issues. The theme of design policy was chosen by the organising committee who decided that the conference should address a wide range of topics of international interest, described by the organisers as the way in which the:

'Growing awareness of critical world problems of natural resources, energy supplies, pollution and the imbalance between rich and poor has led to a wider audience becoming interested in the issues with which design research has been concerned over the past decade. There is an increasing demand for, understanding of, and involvement in, the policy decisions and design processes by which we influence and control our environment – both natural and technological.'

It was clear during the conference that design decisions carry with them important social and political implications. The aim of the conference, to examine the interaction between design and its socio-political context, was made pertinent by the increasing awareness during the conference that the current problems of dealing with rapidly changing technology, world trade depression and unemployment were common to all. There was a belief that there was a necessity for a consensus between government, industry and society concerning the long term aims for the future, and that these aims should be based upon a clear assessment and description of the needs and the courses of action for social and economic change.

Design policy was seen during the conference as operating in a way described by Professor Bruce Archer:

'Design policy will tend to have as its special problem the generalisable, explicatory and social issues arising from the judgemental, creative, productive and specific aspirations of design activity.'

The conference aimed to explore the directions that design research, education, philosophy and practice are taking in this area and to review the development, applicability and potential of design in relation to industry, government, education and social development. This was done by organising the conference in streams. The papers and presentations given on the first day of the conference are published separately under the title *Design Policy: a framework for discussion*. A selection of these papers will also be included in volume 1. The other volumes are:

1 *Design and Society.* Design where the concern is with the decision making at the interface between technology and society.

2 *Design and Industry.* Presenting an international view of the whole of design in industry and its concern with the relationship between design and innovation.

3 *Design Theory and Practice.* Presenting an international review of the state of the art in design theory and the study of design.

4 *Evaluation.* Explaining general schemes for the approach to evaluation for the consumer and society at large. Relevant evaluation constitutes what is likely to be the best guarantee of satisfactory designs and plans.

6 *Design and Information Technology.* Consideration of the current state of the application of information technology in design.

This volume, *Design education*, is concerned with the implications for education. The range of papers presented is described by Ken Baynes in his introduction to this volume and in the paper 'Design education: the basic issue', presented by him and Phil Roberts, who jointly organised this stream. Included in this section are two papers which were presented on behalf of their authors, who at the last moment were unable to attend the conference, which were thought to be worthy of a place in this record of the proceedings. These are 'Design education and economic development' by Anthony Russell and 'Ideas for the development of a curricular system, for teaching design in developing countries' by Arturo Montagu.

The organising committee and the Department of Design Research wish to express their gratitude to those individuals and organisations who assisted generously with their advice and time to make the conference work, and to the participants and contributors for their collective improvement of the understanding and explanation of design policy.

1 Holland, Laurence (ed), *Who Designs America?*, Doubleday, 1966.

Contents

Introduction   5
Ken Baynes and Phil Roberts
Design Education Unit, Royal College of Art, UK

Design education: the basic issues   8
Ken Baynes and Phil Roberts
Design Education Unit, Royal College of Art, UK

Ideas for the development of a curricular system   14
for teaching design in developing countries:
alternatives and contradictions between North
and South hemispheres
Arturo F. Montagu
Institute of Design Research, Faculty of Arts,
University of La Plata, Republic of Argentina

Design education and economic development   23
Anthony K. Russell
School of Art and Design, Western Australian
Institute of Technology

Design for low-income economies   30
Nathan H. Shapira
Department of Art, Design and Art History,
University of California, Los Angeles

Simple design-and-build projects as an aid   36
in teaching engineering design
A. E. Churches
School of Mechanical and Industrial Engineering,
University of New South Wales, Australia

The writing of learning experiences as a   42
teaching tool
G. H. A. van Eyk
School of Industrial Design Engineering,
Delft University of Technology

Experimental design: an antidote to the   46
design process
Avram Grant
Centre for Technological Education, Holon, Israel

Design education for industrial managers   49
Roger A. Gale
Smallpeice Trust Limited, Southampton

Curriculum development in design at further   53
education level
R. C. Sale
Chelsea School of Art, UK

Local curriculum development in environmental   57
education
Eileen Adams
Design Education Unit, Royal College of Art, UK

Analysis and synthesis, the recto and verso   61
of design
Herman Neuckermans
K. U. Leuven – Afdeling Architektuur, Belgium

Cultural-historical awareness: an aspect in   65
the education of industrial designers
Dietmar Palloks
Kunsthochschule Berlin, GDR

Introduction

The aim of the conference was to 'examine the interaction between design and its various contexts: social, political, industrial and environmental. It will review the development, applicability and potential of design in relation to government, industry, education, social development and technological change'.

Clearly, we might think that education has something to say about such matters. But let's move straight away from the kind of language game which might suggest that an abstraction – education – has things to say. In relation to the design education stream of the conference, the intention was to attend to what was said (or not) by practitioners in educational practice. And it is possible to make an 'explanatory' sketch of why many of the participants in the education stream appeared to be some distance from the overall title of the conference, 'Design Policy'.

First of all, many practitioners feel an unease about what they judge – rightly or wrongly – to be the character of many policy statements. More specifically, practitioners may feel that policy statements which are in reference to curricular practices are too frequently prescriptive in character; and as implying the ability of 'education' to deliver against any and all goals which may be set. Further, practitioners may see statements issuing from the policy level of education as being operationally simplistic, as lacking in awareness of their possible and actual curricular enactment. They might feel that there are proper limits to, as well as limitations in, practice; and that, therefore, the expression of unrealistic hopes and the offering of false promises are hindrance rather than help. Thus the overall title, Design Policy, may be construed in a far more specific sense: say, 'Educational Policy in relation to Design'. Certainly that is a shift, but it seems too slight. The participants were, in the main, educational practitioners: that is, the collective view of what was to count as appropriate subject matter for our attention was a reflection of their location and, for many practising teachers, the abstractions of policy level statements (as distinct from courses of action) can seem – how shall we put it? – too distant from the experienced complexities of teaching and learning. Of course this reflects a particular view of policy from a particular base, and indeed that would no doubt be precisely the point.

So from 'Educational Policy in relation to Design', we might propose a further shift. Let's try 'Design-Educational Policy in relation to Design'; it seems to be moving closer to practitioners' perceptions and experience.

So far, perhaps so good. We may still be wrong-footed if we too carelessly join in the game of constructing models of real-life. And then, consequently, perhaps innocently, fall headlong into the trap of supposing that such models necessarily or actually have some kind of equivalence to practitioners' experience and the world of action. But one of the fascinating aspects of the design education stream was that the participants stayed on their own ground. In doing so, they were entirely proper. The significance of this is worth drawing attention to now, because the force of that significance was perhaps no more than indicated during the period of the conference itself. At the risk of creating unwieldly phrases then, the participants in the design education stream addressed themselves, even more specifically, to 'Design Educational Curriculum Policy and Practice'. Unpacked a little, this would suggest, for instance, that participants recognised a distinction between design policy and design educational policy. But it might also suggest the notion of policy and practice being discrete. The separation can be removed by offering a more faithful rendering: 'Design Educational Curriculum Policy-and-Practice'. And the inclusion of 'Curriculum' locates that policy-and-practice. At all events, such a holistic and more specific expression might be a more persuasive notion to practitioners in the field. Such a policy and practice would include the consideration of:

1   the nature of design phenomena (that is, that with which 'designing' treats);
2   the nature of the 'design capacity' and its functioning (that is, that capacity which is necessarily engaged when treating with design phenomena);
3   the nature of developing that capacity (that is, the consideration of design and design educational activity; learning-through-designing; designerly knowledge, understanding, and competences);
4   the developmental 'stages', the needs, the aspirations, of those engaged in learning-through-designing;
5   the diverse and the essentially constraining factors of educational institutions; and
6   the cultural context of design phenomena.

Certainly the participants were concerned with these. But was it possible to give some indications of what might be a *better* curriculum policy and practice? After the event, it is possible to suggest that such a curriculum policy and practice (and in this context we mean one which educational practitioners would recognise as responding to their experience) might necessarily include consideration and action in relation to five areas.

First, it might include the development of teachers' personal and professional competences and responsibilities for the development of pedagogy and courses. A second area for consideration and action might be the encouragement, not the inhibition, of curriculum development both in terms of curriculum action and curriculum theory. In a third area, attention would be drawn to the encouragement, not the

5

inhibition, of the emergence and the development of more appropriate ways of assessing and appraising students' activity. In a fourth area of curriculum policy and practice, consideration and action would be in reference to the range of students engaging in the curricula. Within this area – and easy to say if not necessarily so to achieve – the effect of such attention would tend to be the raising of awareness of the possibility of cultural bias (in whatever direction) in curriculum programmes and proposals. A further effect of such attention would be to raise awareness of the possibility of curricula and curricular proposals displaying a gender bias (in whatever direction). Finally, a better curriculum policy and practice might draw attention to and result in action concerning the possibility of curricular proposals and programmes being too prescriptive in character, and especially to the nature and effects of public examinations.

This may be referred back to the operational curriculum. For instance, it might be worth attempting to articulate criterial questions, questions which could be held against operational curricula and which have particular reference therefore to design and to design educational activity. As a first essay, we could propose a series thus:

Does, or might, experience of (this) curriculum activity develop the student's ability to:

— identify and sufficiently 'define' 'problem situations' based on his own experience (that is, real world, value-laden and ill-defined situations)?
— analyse such conditions and problem-states?
— distinguish between existential and technical problems and discriminate between problems and puzzles?
— propose 'solutions' (or resolutions) to perceived problem states?
— realise a chosen solution (whether or not *function* is to be construed in a narrowly utilitarian or in a self-expressive sense)?
— identify personal and social criteria of 'solutions'?
— identify constraints on their proposals and actions?
— make decisions, and act? ... imagine/calculate the consequences of those decisions and those actions which are to be carried out?
— evaluate the perceived consequences of those actions which are carried out?
— elicit/discover relevant sources and information?
— plan and organise thought, action, media and materials in ways and outcomes appropriate to (1) required functions (whether primarily 'utilitarian' or primarily 'expressive') and (2) contexts?
— perceive the outcomes of design activity, design decisions and choices, in and beyond the world of institutional education, from various role-views of the activity?
— perceive own needs together with the needs of others?

— perceive a necessary balance between traditional and developing technologies, especially in a chosen area or a selected strand of design activity or in relation to particular design phenomena?
— perceive different frameworks (eg economic, cultural) through which design phenomena and design activity may be viewed, and recognise the possible or actual biases of differing cultural views?

All this – that is, the idea of a practitioners' curriculum policy and practice – is not beside the point. For in the light of it, some points may be discerned concerning the papers.

The papers give something of a picture of the practitioners' world, or at any rate parts of a picture of that world as seen by particular practitioners. So it is worth observing that if we seek to engage in discourse, if we seek to appreciate better the state of the field as revealed through some practitioners' utterances, one potential dilemma appears to resolve itself. But perhaps it is a dilemma contingent upon a mistaken (in this context) kind of academic fastidiousness. To achieve a faithful rendering of the state of the practitioners' world it is necessary to listen; and to accommodate accounts which may well include instances of what academic craftsmanship might see, in other circumstances, as partialities, as contentious and tendentious and even not entirely well-informed assertions. If we wish to speak with each other and develop curriculum discourse we attend to what the other says, rather than inform him of what he should have said and instruct him in what he ought to believe. One consequence of the absence of that kind of academic tidying-up is that the papers are extraordinarily interesting to read: there is a certain need for the reader perhaps to adjust his own terminology and certainly a need to spot the underlying theoretic and practical issues of the curriculum. If any defence were needed of the absence of academic tidiness, then it would be that practitioners' accounts may lead us to a better understanding of the complexity, the diversity, and the ambiguities of action; may point to the relations between theory and practice; and to the nature of the linguistics of discourse in relation to the world of action.

The papers offer us a series of accounts or offerings by committed educational practitioners: they are voices from the world of action, not representing the field nor intending to do so. Some take the form of descriptive accounts of cases; others are participant accounts. Still others are meta-activity reflections which focus our attention on specific theoretic and practical issues. For example, the tension between design educational activity leading to greater self-knowledge and, on the other hand, the satisfying of academic-institutional and societal expectations is addressed. Or, 'design methods' re-appear: one man's method is another man's strait-jacket; but to the other, 'method' may be liberating, more or less useful on a take-it-or-leave-it basis. All of the papers are recognisably of the practitioners' world of action, and all, academically speaking, include substantive issues that can be addressed in the field of Design Curriculum Studies. Not all the papers included here were presented at the Conference: much more time would have been needed; and not all those who made presentations at the Conference have been able to produce accounts of their presentations for inclusion. Nevertheless, the papers display the range of the field, and are witness to the strength and the growth of professional discourse in curriculum policy-and-practice.

Phil Roberts
Ken Baynes

Design education: the basic issues

Ken Baynes and Phil Roberts
Design Education Unit, Royal College of Art

The purpose of this paper is to set out briefly some of the crucial streams of thought that have contributed to our present view of design education. It is interesting that, in Britain at least, many of these have first arisen in connection with general education. Perhaps this is because it is here that philosophical and educational issues come up most sharply. The fact is, however, that it is increasingly possible to view design education as a whole, from primary to tertiary, and to see that the same concerns are important throughout the spectrum.

The streams of thought we are dealing with have developed first of all as an historical phenomenon. Many have roots as far back as the Renaissance: some are older still. The industrial revolution represents another moment of critical change and upheaval. In a more immediate sense, the ideas we are dealing with have roots in the art and design experiments of the 1930s, the explosion of the 1960s, the period of student revolt and the subsequent period of retrenchment and increasing bureaucracy. It is not our intention to deal with the history in this paper. That is an important piece of work that still remains to be done. Here our aim is to look at 'the state of the art' as it has developed and to ask: 'what are the ideas and issues for now and the future?'

In presenting this picture we shall draw on work which has been done in and around the Design Education Unit at the Royal College of Art by ourselves and our colleagues.

Design capacity as a fundamental attribute of human beings

At the outset it is necessary to distinguish between two diametrically opposed views of design and designing. These are:

1   That design is highly specialist, complex and esoteric – that particularly the act of designing is something which people can do only after a long apprenticeship;
2   That design ability, like language ability, is something that everyone possesses at least to some degree.

We certainly take the second view. We believe it is the common sense one, borne out by ordinary experience. We hope that in time work now beginning will show just how children first develop a sense of such things as space, how they first begin deliberately to use cognitive modelling, how they first deploy tools and materials in a purposeful way. For the moment, however, we can recognise that in play they *do*, in fact, do all these things, even if we do not yet understand the developmental aspect in any very coherent way. All small children display design ability and use it in their own activities even when it is neglected in formal education. This is hardly surprising because some knowledge of design, however acquired, is needed for survival.

We all, for example:

— try to create an environment which reflects our aspirations;
— use tools and materials purposefully in cooking, do-it-yourself, dressmaking and so on;
— make judgements about which objects and places we like or dislike, even attempting to say why;
— find ourselves moved and excited by fine things that other people have made;
— choose or make clothes which make us feel at ease, which we believe are 'like ourselves';
— respond to the visual messages of advertising, products, signs, buildings, films, television;
— create visual images by photography and make qualitative judgements about which ones are 'successful' or which ones are 'unsuccessful'.

And, of course, we depend on the services of a society which uses all these sorts of ability in a deliberate way. When we carry them out we are, just as with language, creating meaning. We are making up life as we go along. We make up life through buildings, places, products and images just as much as we do through books, scientific enquiry, mathematical symbols, dramatic presentations or sport.

Cognition and cognitive modelling

We have just suggested that design is essentially to do with the ability to conceptualise and evaluate plans for the future. This can be done externally through such familiar mediums as words, drawings, plans, maps, models, prototypes and the like. Professor Archer's important contribution over the last few years has been to show that these external manifestations depend on an internal ability to model known as 'cognitive modelling'. The idea is so central that it is worth spelling out more exactly what is meant by this term.[1]

The term 'cognition' is intended to embrace all those processes of perception, attention, interpretation, pattern recognition, analysis, memory, understanding and inventiveness that go to make up human consciousness and intelligence. Philosophers of mind and cognitive psychologists tend now to talk of cognition as the mental function of construing sense experience as conceptions, and of relating conceptions with one another. The use of the word 'construe' is significant. It is intended to acknowledge the circumstance that the individual conscious being cannot 'know' anything of the reality beyond its own skin except by the collection and interpretation of the signals received by its sense organs. These signals are overlaid by all sorts of irrelevance, interference and noise, and distorted on reception by all sorts of errors, illusory juxtapositions and omissions.

Moreover, in the neurological sense, the signals are ultimately received as electrochemical impulses scattered over different parts of the grey matter of the brain. There is no screen anywhere in the mind on to which a collected picture is projected. The conception in the mind which is built from these scattered impulses is that of a coherent set of signals betraying the presence of a supposedly equally coherent causal phenomenon beyond the sense organs. Subsequent patterns of signals may reinforce or deny the conception, or permit the useful association of conceptions into greater conceptions. When they are sufficiently integrated these constructions in the mind become a general cognitive model of external reality. Since the cognitive model is all the individual consciousness has as evidence of external reality, then for all practical purposes the cognitive model is seen as if it were the reality. Memory and imagination are those further capacities of mind which are capable of conjuring up models of reality in the absence of causative sense data.

There is evidence that the human mind is predisposed to construe sense experience in particular ways, so that conceptions of space, form, object-coherence, colour, temperature, sound and so on, are common to all human beings. These could be called categories of perception. There is also evidence that the human mind is predisposed to seek similarities within and between its accumulating conceptions, and to assign these to categories. It is from the labelling of conceptions and categories, and from the labelling of the relations between conceptions and categories that rational thought springs. It is from the recognition of pattern in and amongst conceptions and in and amongst categories, and from the recognition of pattern amongst the kinds of relations which conceptions and relations have with one another, that 'designerly' thought springs. There is a third predisposition of the human mind which lifts it above and beyond that of other sentient beings. This is the predisposition to assign symbols to represent conceptions, categories and relations. The use of symbols permits abstraction in inner thought, and the externalisation of thought for recording or communication purposes.

In the course of evolution the left half of the human brain has learned to specialise in the arts of categorisation from which is developed rational sequential thought, and in the use of digital symbol systems to construct language, mathematics and forms of notation. At the same time the right half of the human brain has learned to specialise in pattern recognition, and the use of presentational symbol systems to construct images, diagrams and other spatial forms of representation. Interplay between the two halves of the brain permits the pursuit of thought both to the highest levels of abstraction and to the further reaches of practical planning and design.

To return to the issues which gave rise to these notes, the terminology used can be clarified as follows:

The expression 'cognitive modelling' is intended to refer to the basic process by which the human mind construes sense experience to build a coherent conception of external reality and constructs further conceptions of memory and imagination. The expression 'imaging' is intended to refer to that part of cognitive modelling which construes sense data and constructs representations spatially and presentationally, rather than discursively and sequentially.

This picture of the human being has many implications for design education. One of the most dramatic is that it must be an error to identify design as in any special sense 'visual'. To match the cognitive model, it needs to be holistic in its content. To enlarge on this holism it is possible to suggest a range of questions that a twelve-year-old might ask, and for which design activity might provide a focus for discussing, expanding, reflecting and developing meaning. Here they are:

What is the world like?
What am I like?
How did the world come to be the way it is?
How did I come to be the way I am?
How can I look at and analyse the world I live in and understand it?
How can I express or represent what I feel and know about the world?
How do I want to live in the world?
What do I value?
Why do I like what I like?
Can I make the world more like what I like?
Can the world be made better?
Can I improve myself?
How can I plan to improve the world or myself or both?
Do I need to work with other people to improve the world?
How can I work with them?
How can I express or represent my plans?
How can I make my plans become reality?
What tools and materials can I use?
How can I use them?
Must I change my plans because of what I know about tools and materials?
Is what I have made a success?
What do I mean by success?
How do I find out if it is a success?
Do I think it is a success?
Do other people think it is a sucess?
Which is more important – their judgement or mine?
What have I learnt from trying to change the world?
Have I changed?
What do I value?
How do I want to live?
What is the world like?
What am I like?

Clearly, the majority of these questions cannot be said to be only the concern of design. Many are shared with philosophy or ethics, others with art or craft or technology. But a number can only be dealt with by design. And the linkage from introspection, from an understanding of the world as it is, to the decision to act and to grasp that we are changed by acting, is at the core of what design has to offer as an educational experience at any level.

The significance of tool making and using

A number of recent statements, including some originating from the Design Education Unit, have attempted to identify tool making and tool using as the fundamental origins of design and, therefore, at the basis of any design educational experience. It is a view that has caused uneasiness and, in a recent paper for the Unit, Phil Roberts attempted to say in just what ways it is an inadequate position. Since he linked his critique with a reassertion that 'taking action' is the fundamental element, it is worth following it in some detail. Here is a series of extracts:[2]

'The criticism directed by some in-field practitioners towards the asserted fundamentalness of tool-making and tool-using, and their criticism of the degree of significance that is attributed to tool-making and tool-using, presumably imply the belief that there can be articulated a more fundamental and more encompassing model or rationale.

'Or, perhaps the criticism implies that the attribution of paramount significance to tool-making and tool-using is to have displayed a subsidiary model. It says, perhaps, that a particular, but nevertheless "strong", interpretation of the capacity for tool-making and tool-using is actually or potentially partial; and therefore misleading. It is saying, perhaps, that a model that is constituted in the tool-making and tool-using capacity is lacking in explanatory power: it is not sufficiently persuasive.

'Differently put, and perhaps more accurately, it is not tool-using and tool-making that is inadequate: it is, rather, the inadequacies inherent in the conceptions of some practitioners that is weak, and which is demonstrated in some familiar curriculum activities. This is a hard-hitting view; but its basic proposition may be expressed easily enough.

'The proposition is that the capacity for tool-making and tool-using – as commonly understood, and this is an important qualification – does not provide the constituent basis for a powerful model. However, the term "tool-making and tool-using" is descriptive of a dimension of, or a strand in, a quite different conceptualisation. On this view, the status of tool-making and tool-using is translated from constituting a model to being a dimension of a larger conceptual-isation.'

But what is this larger conceptualisation? Phil Roberts continues:

'It is natural for the human animal to wish to "make his mark in and on the world" or to wish to be recognised as "a person". The human animal is so predisposed. This predisposition may be expressed alternatively or additionally in saying that man exhibits a "will to meaning": he wishes, necessarily, to understand himself, others, his habitat, and his place in it. The will to meaning is an aspect of the need of human beings to understand their condition and habitat – inner and external reality.

'In the pursuit of that greater understanding, and through differing kinds of knowing and forms of knowledge, human beings act, individually and collectively, in and on the world. Human beings possess a fundamental capacity: the capacity for, and disposition towards, taking action in and on the world. The capacity to act is exhibited in differing manifestations that employ different modes in relation to distinguishable kinds of phenomena and differing functions.

'The capacity may be displayed in complex collective acts which employ high technologies, and which may be both celebratory and highly functional-operational. This is to suggest that whatever the manifestation, and whatever the mode and medium, the fundamental capacity to which any particular manifestations are in reference is the capacity for action and its associated disposition to take action in and on the world.

On this view, the fundamental conceptualisation is of man as the agent of action, whether this action is to be construed in a context of high technologies or existentially as the necessity to create or find meaning and greater understanding and in-controlness.'

At a later point the paper states the following:

'Parenthetically, it might be worthwhile to attempt to relate this, which is potentially a re-conceptualisation of curriculum, to that familiar phrase, "Doing and making". In practice, the phrase almost always carries, as understood, a "necessary" conjunction with artefacts: "making (some artefact)". But on the view expressed above, the term requires extension. The term is too narrowly and too partially operational, and lacking in the human dimension. It may be extended thus: "Doing, making, and being = acting in and on the world", or, man the agent of intentional action.

'Hence the status of artefacts, in an educational context, is opened up to possible re-appraisal. A model of artefact achieving is obviously legitimate when artefact achieving is the principal objective. But once it is conceded that a model of artefact achieving is not synonymous with a model of educational intent and practice, then the possible re-appraisal of the status of artefacts raises questions to do with the nature of the relations between (1) the development of the agent of action; (2) the development of mind; and (3) the achieving of artefacts.

'To summarise:
Let it be accepted that man-the-agent-of-action provides the fundamental conceptualisation on which educational rationales, practices, and specific models of action might be more appropriately premised.

'Let real-world ill-defined problems represent the phenomena with which man the agent of action necessarily treats.

'Let it be accepted that the nature of human being in the world (or being a person) is necessarily at the core of any putative "explanation" of human action.

'Let us call the capacity for intentional action the design capacity: that is, the design capacity is constituted in the capacity for and predisposition towards taking intentional and mindful action.

Then the development of that capacity, employed and engaged-in when treating with ill-defined problems, is central to would-be educative practice. The capacity to act with intention is realised and manifested in the functioning of "cognitive modelling". In treating with real-world ill-defined problems, cognitive modelling engages, employs, and is constituted in, differing modes of conceptualising, symbolising, and presentational systems, according to the subject phenomena, the "task situation", and the required functions/purposes. The operations encompassed by the term "cognitive modelling" are necessarily and inevitably complex, inter-active, and transformational. Different curriculum subjects, or curriculum areas, are intended to provide opportunities which will have the effect of developing the capacity to act, both in a general sense and in terms of specific kinds of action and in relation to particular kinds of phenomena.'

The concept of literacy

When we turn to see the design capacity in a social and cultural framework, then the concept of literacy becomes important. This, however, is a somewhat misused term, and it is necessary to say first what we intend by it.

The word literacy is much in vogue. Curriculum documents refer to such concepts as 'visual literacy' or 'technological literacy'. It is not always clear what people mean by this. Sometimes it seems that all they mean is that children and adults should spend more of the school or college day on whatever subject they are advocating. This is beside the point. Literacy has a little to do with the acquisition of knowledge or skills in a narrow sense: rather it is about the growth of attitudes and confidence that will lead to participation: to, once again, the ability to 'take action' and be 'in control'.

In a brilliant article, 'Classic Culture and Post-culture', George Steiner has made very clear the difference between being able to read and write and being literate in a larger sense. In the following extract he is discussing the background against which authors wrote in what he describes as the 'classical age of the book' between 1730 and 1885:[3]

'The consensus of echo on which the authority and effectiveness of books depended went deeper than schooling. A corpus of agreed reference is in fact of philosophic, social value. The economy of statement that makes possible a literary style, and the recognizable challenges to that style by the individual writer, has underlying it a large sum of undeclared but previously agreed-to social and psychological assumptions. This is especially so of the high literacy between the times of Montesquieu and of Mallarmé. The kind of lettered public they had in view is directly expressive of an agreed social fabric. Both the linguistic means and the range of matter of books – in short the semantic whole of authorship and reading – embodied and helped perpetuate the hierarchic power relations of western society.'

Steiner's concept of 'the semantic whole' as a bond between writers and readers and their sharing of a common frame of reference is something which we can also recognise in, for example, architectural design in the eighteenth century. But it would be wrong to assume, as Steiner seems to assume, that such 'semantic wholes' only have validity in the setting of aristocratic culture. We can see exactly the same gripping involvement in the creation of jazz in New Orleans or the jokes and songs which children tell themselves in the school playground.

In art and design the situation is particularly teasing. There is no 'semantic whole' between painters and sculptors and the mass of the public, and there is positive war between architects and planners and the people who live in the flats, houses and towns that they have created. Yet these experts are the accredited, professional guardians of design awareness. In these circumstances what can a concept like literacy mean, and how could it be brought about?

The simple answer must be that we do not know what literacy in design might mean because we have not yet experienced it in a mass industrial society. What we can say, I think, is that they are not 'semantic wholes' that can be created by a change that affects only one side of the equation. Steiner provides us with the clue: literacy is something that involves writer and reader in an active partnership. It is not a situation where the writer remains untouched by the encounter. It is a situation where writer and reader interact with one another and, as a result, build up 'a set of philosophic, social values'.

Could such a thing happen as a result of design educational activity? It is not impossible. Already the practice and experience of design work in schools has been separated from blindly copying professional designers. Teachers have been able to provide a wider framework of values than designers are normally able to consider in their day-to-day activities. Some of this thinking could seep into professional practice and those who have experienced it will be at home with it. In a similar way, the Art and the Built Environment Project has provided a place where architects and planners have been able to join with teachers and children in a deliberate attempt to educate one another. Within the tiny compass of the 'semantic whole' provided by a course or conference it has been remarkable to watch the development of shared languages and the ability to think new thoughts.

How relevant is design education?

We have tried to show that the design capacity is fundamental to human beings, that through cognitive modelling it is involved in the great enterprise of 'taking action', of being 'in control'. We have suggested that socially and culturally the goal must be to increase participation and to create a 'semantic whole' between the equivalent of writers and readers – designers and users. We believe that these concepts and arguments hold together and that they provide the beginnings of a framework within which design educational activity can be planned, implemented, discussed and developed.

There remains, however, another dimension to the discussion. And that is to make it clear that, in an historical perspective, design is not just a desirable educational priority – it is a critical one. We are at a point where the deliberate development of the design ability may actually be important for survival.

It can be convincingly argued that 'design education' is simply the most recent form of one of the oldest concerns of education. It is a particular response to the conditions in which we now live, but this does not mean that education in the past ignored design. Education has always concerned itself with material culture as well as with literary and scientific culture. If specific labels are ignored, it is easy to see that what is today known as design education can trace its ancestry back to mankind's very first attempts to create shelter, tools, images and utensils.

There are, however, important qualitative differences between societies dependent on craft-based means of production and those where industrialisation is complete. These differences highlight the significance of design and clarify its role as a mediator between technology and culture. It is worth attempting to trace out these differences rather precisely.

We have now lived through nearly two hundred years of industrialisation. Its effects are widespread in spiritual as well as material things. With this as a social and historical context, it is possible to list some of the reasons why it is important to study design in primary and secondary schools, business colleges, universities and the like, as well as in design schools:

1   Design, in the broadest sense, is the bundle of techniques, skills and approaches that can be used to determine the future character of the man-made world of buildings, places, images and products. Industrialisation has vastly increased the effect of this activity on the quality of life. It now affects everyone.
2   Democracy demands that everybody has an effective say in the decisions which determine the future pattern of social life. But such an idea can only be effective if education can bring alive the issues involved and develop ways in which non-specialists can study them.
3   Technology has vastly enlarged the scope and scale of man's impact on the natural environment. The decisions taken can have a direct effect on the future survival of the planet. The issues are far from simple or clear cut. Design activity is one medium which can provide practice in dealing with the types of open-ended problem that are involved.
4   Technology has ushered in a period of continuing change. Handling change in a purposeful way is one of the main characteristics of design activity. It is important for individual and social survival to be able to control change and to foresee its qualitative results.
5   Mass production has divided the consumer from the maker. The consumer needs a broad range of skills and understanding before he or she can really take control of his or her own environment. An experience of design, which inevitably involves taking qualitative decisions between various alternatives, will help people return a personally valid answer to the question: 'how do I want to live?'
6   Most people react without much thought to the powerful and technologically broadcast visual messages of the media. Yet these affect personal attitudes and inter-personal relationships as well as providing entertainment. They are all produced by design activity and a direct understanding of what is involved will help to develop a more critical and discriminating attitude towards them.

Here are the areas where literacy in our field would need to be effective. Here is where it needs to achieve dramatic changes in the balance of power between designers and users, between provision and participation. Literacy would indicate a general ability to understand and a willingness to take part in this crucial area of human activity: the enterprise of adapting our environment to our spiritual and material needs and, to that degree at least, being 'in control' and creating our own futures. We see that as the underlying aim of all design educational activity.

References

1   Archer, Bruce, internal memo; Royal College of Art, Design Education Unit, 1981.
2   Roberts, Phil, 'Notes towards the articulation of the bases of the design dimension of the curriculum', *Design Examinations at 16+: Discussion and Proposals,* Royal College of Art, Design Education Unit, London.
3   Steiner, George, 'Classic culture and post-culture', *Times Literary Supplement,* October 1971.

Ideas for the development of a curricular system for teaching design in developing countries: alternatives and contradictions between North and South hemispheres

Arturo F. Montagu
Member of the National Research Council CONICET
Institute of Design Research, Faculty of Arts,
University of La Plata, Republic of Argentina

In the last five years we have developed alternative design experiments with students and designers in Belgium,[1] France,[2] and Argentina[3] seeking new design methodologies to deal with facts and events that occur in most developing countries[4] in order to find new types of design solutions that could fit more properly into this part of the world which has little chance of survival if we are not able to develop a strategical action for the amelioration of the physical and psychological environment.

The objective of this paper is to present an introduction which discusses the potential subjects (globally) that should be included in a curricular system. Two are case studies of projects for the design of villages including a re-design of arts and crafts on the Ivory Coast in West Africa and the Argentinian and Bolivian 'Altiplano' in Latin America as examples of the type of design strategy for pragmatical solutions that should be introduced in design schools in developing countries.

Introduction

The traditional approach to teaching design (urban, architectural and industrial) using a combinatorial strategy of: 'Bauhaus-Ulm' methods – W. Gropius,[5] M. Bill,[6] T. Maldonado;[7] 'the system methodologies of the 1960s – B. Archer,[8] G. Broadbent,[9] J.C. Jones,[10] S.A. Gregory;[11] 'the user participation alternatives' of the 1970s; J.N. Habraken;[12] also in the 1970s the 'integrated design' concept by V. Papanek;[13] also in the same decade, as in the next one, the beginning of the 'Post Modern' actions and proposals[14] and the 'Styling' approach of the Americans [15] are no longer enough to cope with the problems which affect most developing countries mainly in the Southern hemisphere.

For people living in the villages of Gezira (Sudan),[16] in the mountains of Tarija (Bolivia)[17] or in the dramatic landscape of Bangladesh, most of the 'Gute form' products, artifacts and environmental functionalistic ideas produced by Western technology do not fit properly with the roots and anthropological patterns of these cultures.

The first working hypothesis of this paper endeavours to develop a basic methodology for the pattern recognition of cultures in agrarian or pre-industrial societies in order to see if it is possible to adapt any of the proposals stated here.

C. Levi-Strauss[18] says: 'We (Europeans), have been taught from infancy to be self-centred and individualistic, "to fear the impurity of foreign things", a doctrine which we embody in the formula: "Hell is others" (L'enfer, c'est les autres), but primitive myth has the opposite moral implication: "Hell is ourselves".'

It is essential to assume that one of the main points to understand the mental structure of ethnic groups in developing countries, is to take into consideration the way in which they act, think and express themselves by means of myths, language, rituals, arts and crafts, building, cooking, dance, etc. for organising their deteriorated but integrated environment.

'Primitive people are no more mystical in their approach to reality than we are. The distinction rather is between a logic which is constructed out of observed contrasts in the sensory qualities of concrete objects eg: the difference between: raw and cooked, wet and dry, centre and periphery, and a logic which depends upon the formal contrasts of entirely abstract entities eg $+$ and $-$ or $\log x$ or x^e. The latter kind of logic is a different way of talking about the same kind of thing'.[19]

Therefore it will neither be technology, nor the adequate use of methodologies, nor the development of arts and crafts, nor methods of green revolution to improve agricultural production that will enable improvement of the present situation, if we are unable to understand the basic characteristics of each ethnic group and adapt these characteristics to present and future needs.

In recent years it has been possible to observe individual reactions by sensible young designers[20,21,22,23] working some time together with anthropologists and rural sociologists[24,25] presenting some alternative views of this problem, but certainly there does not exist an organised and structural strategy for teaching design in developing countries, nor in those schools which are well adapted to highly industrialised countries and wish to understand the problems in the Southern hemisphere.[26]

The idea is not of course a romantic return to nature like the pseudo-paradise retreats shown in cartoons, or to act by using a patronising attitude to produce another vicious circle of dependency on foreign ideas and technology; but to show in rational terms the profound misfits which affect the design activity in most developing countries.

The underdeveloped world

Facts and figures
'Underdevelopment may be defined as a situation in which nations, groups and individuals have little or no power to decide upon their own development.

'Economically: it is characterised by an inability to utilise available resources making use of suitable technologies for the satisfaction of human needs. *'Socially*: this inability is linked with deficient or irrelevant education, poor health and inadequate social security.

'*Politically*: underdevelopment is generally associated with a lack of genuine autonomy.

'Thus underdevelopment may be regarded as a relative concept defined by options and restrictions in a given historical situation.'[27]

This definition of an 'underdeveloped world', quoted from SAREC, the Swedish Agency for Research and Co-operation with developing countries, has given a synthetic and specific description of the problem which will help to find a starting point for a strategical action in order to succeed in achieving the main objective of this paper, the curricular system, based on a real and logical sequence of principles and possibilities.

There are also other definitions of the problem which might help us to go into more detail as expressed in '*North–South: a Programme for Survival*'.

'A people aware of their cultural identity can adopt and adapt elements true to their value-system and can thus support an appropriate economic development. There is no uniform approach, there are different and appropriate answers depending on history and cultural heritage, religions, traditions, human and economic resources, climatic and geographic conditions, and political patterns of nations. But there is a common notion that cultural identity gives people dignity.'[28]

There are figures and facts provided by United Nations statistics[29] which represent dramatically the relationship between parameters as GDP (Gross Domestic Product) of the North and South hemispheres.

There are other variables, such as energy, raw materials, health, education and housing, that will affect directly any potential solution.

The symbolic world

Apart from these overwhelming facts, we must enter a field in which the experience of designers is little, and this field deals with how primitive cultures build up their symbolic world in terms of relative concepts of space and time, which in fact involve the concept of limit.

Thus we as designers and teachers, if we are not able to understand how decodified are those limits, and the myths and rituals which organise the social life of each ethnic group in the 118 developing countries, will find it very difficult to transfer any type of knowledge (technical, social, economic, etc) to those countries.

Leach[30] provided us with a strong argument: 'Our capacity to divide the outer world into categories of names and, at a later stage, organise these

categories to adapt them to our social convenience, depends on the fact that though our capacity to modify the outer environment is very limited, we have virtually an unlimited capacity to play with our inner version of the environment in our minds.'

And this is the main problem for the development of the curricular system. We must be able to modify and adapt this internally accepted concept of the environment which normally, for most designers in the Western world, belongs to a rational-functionalistic approach of the solutions, into a more particular and adaptable vision to build up the environment in agrarian and pre-industrial societies.

Therefore we should be able to understand the myths, the signals and the symbols of those cultures, otherwise there will be a continuous misplacement of people and technology, just because it is impossible to see the type of 'gradual' and 'possible' solutions adapted specially to each particular situation in the environment areas of developing countries.

Contradictions and oppositions

What is needed is a change or a different attitude for organising the curricular systems of design schools showing a possible pattern to reduce the risk of what is happening now in developing countries where design education is rather critical in terms of resolving the urgent problems in the areas of housing, health, education, transportation, etc.

Our suggestion is that a set of oppositions (see Figure 1, overleaf) existing at present should be analysed because these are the causes of many misfits in the urban and rural zones in the Southern hemisphere.[31] Each component of the opposition list is represented globally by a set of variables that could act as parts of a very open system that will help to establish a synchronic vision of the problem.

The left side of this opposition list is well known by most Western designers, but the right side of it is less known, not only by Western designers but by designers living in developing countries also.

The misfits are basically political, economic and technological, and the interaction among them affects directly the inmediate environment of man.

As is possible to observe in Figure 1, the relations among two or more variables allow a potential field of study to be detected which could first be allocated to one of the global phases and later converted or adapted into a particular subject or theme for the curricular system.

It is possible to assume that this methodology could be interpreted as a system view of the problem, but of

SET OF OPPOSITIONS (figure I)

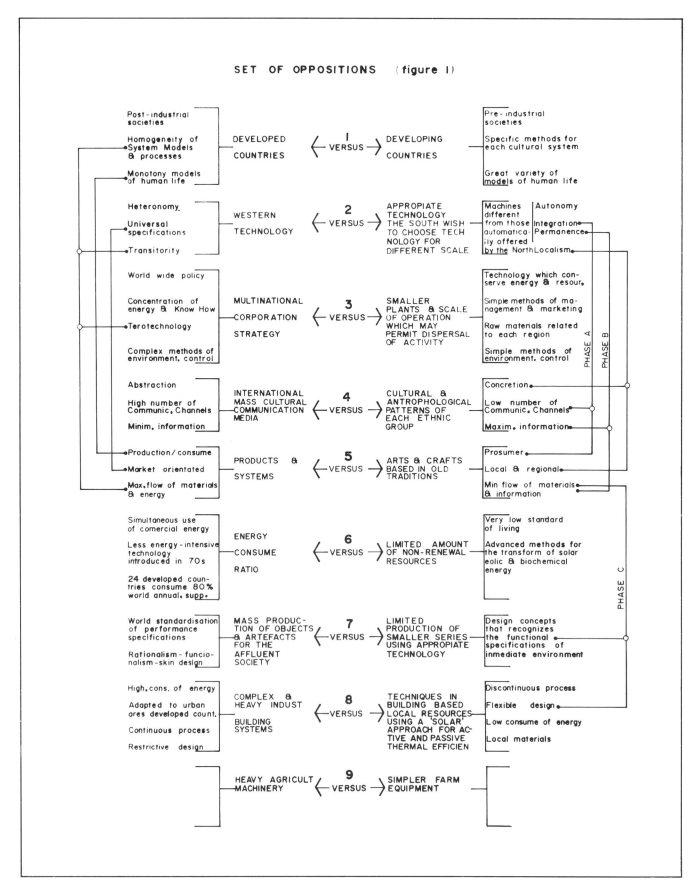

course there are some differences, because the set of oppositions are acting here as a synchronic section of the problem at the beginning of the 1980s decade, but what would be necessary is to adapt diachronically[32] the set of oppositions to each cultural system in each developing country along a period of time.

The system view mentioned before allows us to distinguish three basic sub-systems: the 'technological subs ' (oppositions 2–5, 6–9); the 'sociological subs ' (oppositions 1–4) and the 'ideological subs ' (opposition 3).

The set of relations which inter-relate these sub-systems are particular to each culture; it is also noted that the dominant sub-system is the technological one, and without being technocrats it is possible to assume for the second hypothesis of this paper, that technological development through 'appropriate design' should be the important matter to develop in the curricular system.

Finally it would be convenient to be clear about the third hypothesis of this paper concerning the need for taking advantage of the great technological progress of the Northern hemisphere, because this technological progress conveniently put through the relations of the sociological sub-system could produce great benefits in the South.[33]

Curricular system

Models of education

The correlation between the contradictions of the social systems and the relative impotence of the education models is evident. The vicious circle of economic underdevelopment and the misadjustment of several education models could be broken by establishing a 'development strategy on both sides of the problem', which is the fourth hypothesis of this work.

Apparently 'motivation' is the key point of every modern education policy and Western models of education are based on two principal objectives: education for learning and future teaching; and education for obtaining a job.[34]

But when these models are applied mainly to agrarian or pre-industrial societies they produce negative consequences as a by-product of the incompatibility of the state of development of these groups.

The fifth working hypothesis for future applications of the curricular system is that the state of social development of each ethnic group should be first analysed, before thinking of the transference of any type of knowledge.

It is perfectly known that it is not only the postgraduate design students coming from pre-industrial societies to developed ones to study, who suffer a profound sense of misfit because of the strong difference in the way systems, models and processes are carried out in the North.

Experimental Model for Design Education: EMDE

In accordance with the great variety of cultural patterns that can be observed in Third World countries, it is suggested here that it is necessary to define the curricular system by means of a set of phases globally, in order to be adapted to each ethnic group in each developing country.

Therefore, it would be necessary to act in a completely different way, to take into consideration simultaneously, and at different levels of complexity, all the components of a new educational structure which is proposed here as the 'Experimental Model for Design Education'.

The idea of EMDE (Figure 2, overleaf) as a model, provides us with a neutral tool, flexible enough to be adapted to most agrarian or pre-industrial societies, showing a structure which could relate the concept of 'ecodevelopment',[35] with the ideas of 'integrated environment'[36] by means of a design methodology plugged into these concepts, and not as an artificial instrument or meta-language.

Looking again at Figure 1 it is possible to observe a set of possible relations among variables on both sides of the list; these relations show a flow of information that is sometimes fluid, and at other times non-existent (a typical weakness in most developing countries).

Nevertheless these relations are the mechanism to detect problems allocated in the several phases, which constitute the basic structure of EMDE and make it possible to define the specific subjects of the curricular system.

Each of these phases have direct connotations with the design activity. It is possible to think that in some way they are in fact very similar to what happens in modern societies in the West, but there is a fundamental difference.

In Western developed countries people can 'choose' products, houses, transport systems, energy systems, holiday systems, and so on. But in developing countries people do not have this chance.

This means that a future designer for the Southern hemisphere cannot think in terms of 'separate' components or products, because there is no demand for such 'products'; instead it should think in terms of 'integrated factors' that can contribute to organise the highly deteriorated physical environment observed in most developing countries, putting aside the personal preference for 'international' forms, materials and technologies, and seek a completely new type of 'conceptual creativity'.[37]

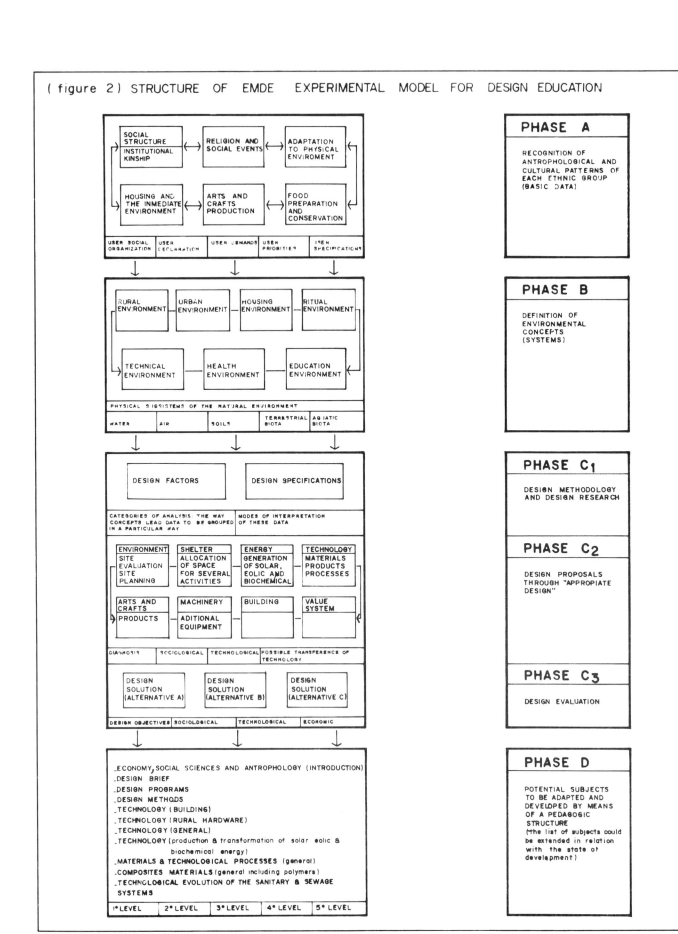

(figure 2) STRUCTURE OF EMDE EXPERIMENTAL MODEL FOR DESIGN EDUCATION

PHASE A

RECOGNITION OF ANTROPHOLOGICAL AND CULTURAL PATTERNS OF EACH ETHNIC GROUP (BASIC DATA)

PHASE B

DEFINITION OF ENVIRONMENTAL CONCEPTS (SYSTEMS)

PHASE C₁

DESIGN METHODOLOGY AND DESIGN RESEARCH

PHASE C₂

DESIGN PROPOSALS THROUGH "APPROPIATE DESIGN"

PHASE C₃

DESIGN EVALUATION

PHASE D

POTENTIAL SUBJECTS TO BE ADAPTED AND DEVELOPED BY MEANS OF A PEDAGOGIC STRUCTURE (the list of subjects could be extended in relation with the state of development)

Conclusions

Certainly the dialogue between the North and the South hemispheres has become increasingly more difficult. There is a gap, widening each year, between the types of plans promoted by developed countries, and the real conditions of dynamic strategy needed by Third World countries to develop themselves.

Nevertheless our aim is that there should be a positive integration between the great amount of design knowledge existing in the North with the increasing difficulties it is possible to observe in the South.

It is not necessary to hold a radical political vision of the problem in order to re-establish equilibrium. What is suggested here is that it should be understood properly which are the 'real' problems facing now half the population of the world and organise rapid actions through governments and international organisations (UNESCO, UNIDO, OEA, CODESTRIA, etc) using education as a tool to improve social conditions, and design education as a tool to improve environmental conditions, and this is the main objective of this study.

References

1 Nationaal Hoger Instituut voor Bouwkunst en Stedebouw, Antwerpen, Belgium (National Institute for Architecture Urbanism & Design), during 1978–80–81.
2 UDRA, Unité de Recherche Appliquée, under supervision of Dominique Clayssen.
3 Institute of Design Research, Faculty of Arts, University of La Plata, Argentina, since 1976.
4 Division for Economic and Social Information. *Towards a World Economy That Works*, United Nations, New York, 1980. According to this publication: of the more than 4 billion people living in the world today, over 70 per cent live in 118 developing countries.
5 Bayer, H., Gropius, W., Gropius, I. *Bauhaus 1919–1928*, C. T. Branford, Boston, 1952.
6 Bill, M. 'Belleza proveniente della funzione e belleza como funzione', in *Domus* no 250, September 1950, p 15.
7 Maldonado, T. *Disegno Industriale: Un riesame, definizieone, Bibliografia,* Feltrinelli, Milan, 1976.
8 Archer, B.L. 'Systematic Method for Designers', in *Design*, April 1963, pp 46–9, June, pp 70–3, August pp 52–7, November pp 68–72.
9 Broadbent, G. *Design in Architecture. Architecture and the Human Sciences*, J. Wiley, London, 1974.
10 Jones, J.C. *Design Methods. Seeds of Human Future*, J.Wiley, 1970.
11 Gregory, S.A. *The Design Method*, Butterworths, London, 1966.
12 Habraken, J.N. *The Supports and People*, Architectural Press, London, 1972.
13 Papanek, V. *Design for the Real World*, Thames & Hudson, London, 1972.
14 Jencks, C. *The Language of Post Modern Architecture*, Academy, London, 1977.
15 Loewy, R. *Industrial Design*, Blume, Barcelona, 1980.
16 Founou-Tchuigova, 'The Facto Wage-Earners in the Gezira Scheme', in *Africa Development, CODESTRIA*, Vol III no 1, Dakar, 1978, pp 25–50.'
17 Ministerio de Asuntos Campesinos, *Mapa Ecologico de Bolivia*, 1976.
18 Leach, E. *Levi-Strauss*, Fontana Modern Masters, 1970, p 37.
19 Leach, E. *op cit*, p 85.
20 Gomez, M.A. *Towards a strategy for design education in developing countries*, Master thesis, Department of Design Research, RCA, London, 1975.
21 Trejo, C., Celiz, C. Postgraduate students from Mexico, at the Industrial Design course of the RCA, winners of the Braun Design Prize 1980.
22 Weil, D. Postgraduate student, at the Industrial Design course of the RCA, London.
23 Lopez, M.J. Postgraduate design student, at the Department of Design Research, RCA, London.
24 Blanco, R., Denegri, R., Ferraris, O., Montagu, A.F. *Design experiments on conceptual creativity*, working paper, Institute of Design Research, Faculty of Arts, University of La Plata, 1977–80.
25 Montagu, A.F., Denegri, R., Ferraris, O. *The design of autonomous rural communities in the north of Argentina*, working paper, Institute of Design Research, Faculty of Arts, University of La Plata.
26 Peters, A. *The Peters Projection*, new world map by Dr Peters of Bremen University introduces several

innovations which represent an important improvement on the prevailing Eurocentric geographical and cultural concept of the world.

27 Anyang Nyongo 'Review of SAREC report 1975–76', in *Africa Development CODESTRIA*. vol III no 1, Dakar 1978, pp 76–79.

28 Independent Commission on International Development Issues, *North-South: a Programme for Survival*, p 24, MIT Press, 1980.

29 Division for Economic and Social Information, *Towards a World Economy That Works, op cit*.

30 Leach, E. *Cultura y Comunicacion*, SIGLO XXI, Mexico, 1978, p 49.

31 Most of the data of the oppositions list are derived and influenced by the following books: *North-South: a Programme for Survival, op cit, Design and Technology* by Nigel Cross (Open University 1975), *The Third Wave* by Alvin Toffler (V. Morrow, 1980). *Small is Beautiful* by Dr. E.F. Schumacher (Abacus 1975), *Small is Powerful* by J. Christopher Jones (Futures Feb. 1981), *Ecol Operation* by Alvaro Ortega (McGill University 1972), Fathy, H. *Architecture for the Poor* by H. Fathy (University of Chicago Press 1973).

32 Leach, E. Levi-Strauss, *op cit*, p 94.

33 We want to mention here the works and projects carried out by the original Intermediate Technology Group based in London and inspired by ideas of Dr. E.F. Schumacher.

34 Faure, E. and others, *Learn to Be*, UNESCO, 1972.

35 Sachs, I. *Pour une Politique du Developpement,* Flammarion, Paris, 1977.

36 Montagu, A.F., Weil, D., Denegri, R., Ferraris, O., *Rural Environment System*, Basic Documents, XIII World Congress of Architects, Mexico 1978, pp 368–373, also published as a summary in *Domus* no 614, p4, 1981. This paper shows the concept of Integrated Environment using the design of a rural community as an example of the type of relations between factors that should be taken in consideration.

37 Patfoort, G.A. 'Il Cimento della Armonia e della Invenzione' in *NEUF* no 88, Professor Patfoort worked intensively mainly in Belgian universities and Third World countries as a UNIDO expert, with the concepts of innovation, creativity, invention and imagination related to materials and technological processes.

Appendix A

Design experiments performed at the Institute of Design Research, Faculty of Arts, University of La Plata, Argentina.

The design of an autonomous rural community in the north of Argentina, near the border of Bolivia.

Figure 3.
Adaptation to the physical environment and considerations about site planning and site evaluation including landscape integration.

Design of houses using traditional building materials

of the region, but adapted and improved (stones, stabilised adobe with cement or asphalt precasted, etc). It is possible to observe also the components for the generation of energy (solar, eolic, biochemical).

Figure 4.
It is possible to observe the way houses are grouped and related to the components for the generation of energy.

This figure shows an alternative design of houses using a different kind of building technology based on precast earth cement.

Appendix B

Design experiments performed at the Nationaal Hoger Instituut voor Bouwkunst en Stedebouw, Product Development Section, Antwerp, 1980.

Figure 5.
Design for the autonomy of a small village beside the sea by fourth year students: E. Van Handenhoven, B. Bacarne, B. Van Sompele. Figure 5 shows the site layout with detached dwellings and the communal building.

Figure 6.
Each dwelling includes a greenhouse for light vegetables and the generation of heat.

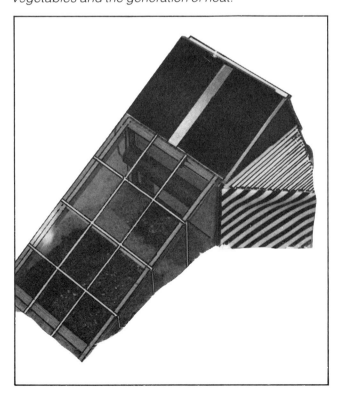

Figure 7.
A mechanical system for the generation of energy using the movement of sea waves.

Appendix C

Design experiments performed at the Nationaal Hoger Instituut voor Bouwkunst en Stedebouw, Product Development Section, Antwerp, Belgium, 1981.

Figure 8.
Learning to recognise anthropological and cultural patterns in a pre-industrial society from Ivory Coast, West Africa.

Possible adaptations to a more rational production process using a scale model of a typical chair (Anthropological Museum, Antwerp).

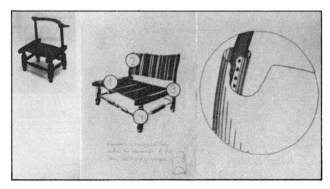

Figure 9.
*This exercise is part of the design of a technical
environment performed by fourth year students.*

*The exercise is organised by means of an 'operative
group technique' which allows fast results. It is a
dynamic method of testing the hypothesis mentioned
in this paper, including the Experimental Model for
Design Education – EMDE.*

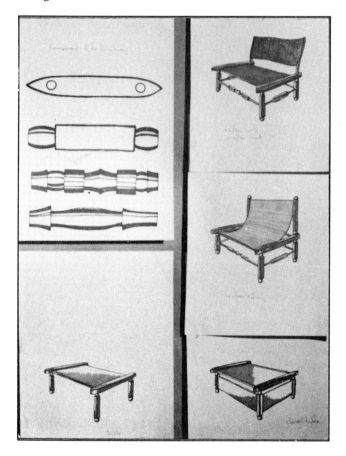

Design education and economic development

Anthony K. Russell

Corresponding Professor, Royal College of Art, UK;
Head, School of Art and Design, Western Australian
Institute of Technology; Deputy National Chairman,
Industrial Design Council of Australia; sometime
UNESCO/UNDP Expert, Design Education

*This paper examines the Design in General Education
Movement, its history of development to date and the
implications of these critical educational initiatives and
experiments for developing Third World countries. It
also reflects on some causes of the misrepresentation
and distortions of the basic assumptions underlying
the fundamental objectives of the educational activity.
It posits that its success or failure, as an important
contribution to the future well-being of mankind, will
require the elimination of the political, economic and
technological imperatives which currently intervene in
and dominate its transmission as an educational
model. It then proposes that a balanced, critical and
objective documentation of both its achievements and
problems of implementation should be made
immediately available to all international agencies for
educational development as a significant contribution
to meaningful Design Policy in a global context.*

Design in general education: success or failure?

The 'Design in General Education Movement' has
become well known to educators outside this country
even though it has some distance to go before it could
claim to have achieved a general acceptance in the
elementary and secondary schools by traditional arts
and crafts teachers. The seminal contributions of a
number of its important theorists and practitioners
have been very enthusiastically received by educators
and designers working outside this country, including
Australians, and there is some evidence to suggest
that the new educational initiatives are likely to interest
people now working in far less developed countries.

I think there is little question that some of this interest is
based on the apparently reforming and thoroughly
modernising potential the activity projects in an
important area of the curriculum which has been sadly
neglected for a long time. Unlike many early reforming
movements concerned with the visual and operational
arts in elementary and secondary education, these
new approaches seem to have a greater social
relevance for our technological and planned society.
This confers on them a probability of acceptance by
those who seek to influence education in ways which
make it more responsive to the functional and rational
objectives of the new society and particularly to the
notions of economic accountability.

This, I believe, represents a serious distortion of the
original and fundamental philosophy and objectives
but it is a very persuasive and attractive doctrine.

Does the movement represent a contemporary reassertion of the earlier 'heroic age' of design when, to
be a designer, meant being part of the rebuilding of a
world shattered by war and a sharing in the
excitement of creating a brave new society? Can we in
truth be satisfied with what has been achieved since
'design', and more specifically the notion of 'good
design' entered the everyday language and became

one of the criteria by which a healthy, vigorous and
creative new human society might be measured?
Design has served the interests and objectives of
modern manufacturing economies, and has made its
contribution to achieving that magical panacea for
economic progress, promoted by economic theorists,
the healthy gross national product. Whether or not the
oft quoted concern for the social and human
consequences of 'good design' has in fact contributed
to the solving of the fundamental human problems and
needs of the world is something else again.

The movement re-examined

There is little doubt that the emergence of the new
initiatives was strongly influenced by a widespread
dissatisfaction among educators and some
distinguished designers, with the way in which design
as a fundamental creative process of mind had failed
to win acceptance in the cultural thinking climate of
the schools in general and in the adult society. At
best, in the highly instrumental 'real world' context, it
had broadened the base of that ephemeral subject
called art appreciation and, for some teachers,
provided a quasi-technical, quasi-scientific
justification for the visual arts in schools in place of the
apologist stance that had so long depressed these
activities in the general education curriculum.

It is not my purpose to dwell at length on these matters
but it is useful to the theme I wish to develop to
summarise some of the significant attitudes of
educators towards design in education.

Collaborators, contextualists and essentialists

The movement has elicited a wide range of responses
and reactions among teachers at all levels of
education. While one of the guiding philosophies and
objectives of the infant movement saw the activity in
education as holistic, interdisciplinary and indivisible,
much of this understanding was subsequently lost or
distorted, chiefly because of the basic pre-
dispositions of the teachers themselves.

The most instrumental and allegedly most materialistic
or opportunistic developments of the activity by
teachers have largely resided in that most badly
neglected field of the arts, the manual arts or 'heavy
crafts', as some describe them. Here the prospect of
modernity being achieved through the enabling
'methodology' of industrial design based largely on
the exemplars provided by the professional, artefact
creating model, was irresistible. For many other arts
and crafts educators this enthusiastic embrace of
'design for a purpose' by their erstwhile colleagues
represented a capitulation to the anaesthetic
processes of the prevailing materialistic culture. In this
sense these teachers were seen as *collaborators* with
the increasingly functional, rational and materialistic
objectives of education in the planned, technological
society.

Teachers whose professional training in the visual or 'Fine Arts' had made them naturally suspicious of the objectivism of design regarded these forms of collaboration not only as antithetic to the concept and ideology of the hard won 'new art education', but a sinister threat to the survival of that activity in a society so deeply enamoured of scientism and technology.

Their *essentialist* view of the arts, rooted firmly in the events that followed upon the acknowledgement of the centrality of art in the development of the young child, almost totally excluded the possibilities of the new movement on the basis of this particular distortion of its aims and objectives.

Paradoxically, in their rejection of the significance of culturally given skills in visual and operational arts education, artist–teachers of the essentialist persuasion seem to have adopted as their own adult model of art, the work of 'infantile artists'. So most contemporary art students, as distinct from many craft and most design students, have grown up with an impoverished sense of reality and an inbuilt incapability for acting upon and affecting the real, lived-in experience of their own society. The Fine Artists today, tragically, appear to have very little to offer the ordinary man and so they, no less than those they criticise as collaborators, have also betrayed the aesthetic, feeling and imagining dimension of ordinary human experience.

Somewhere between these two extreme interpretations and distortions of the movement and its objectives lie the educators with an uncomfortable foot in either camp. In so much as they see the activity as part of a continuum of creative processes and the whole as a part of the essential, ordinary, lived-in experience of person, their stance is *contextual* in nature, the reasonable middle ground.

The professional view of the design activity

The reaction of educators in the specialised tertiary and vocational sector of education to the movement has been predictably antagonistic. It has ranged from a calculated and demoralising expression of indifference on the one hand to a testy refutation of its credibility or validity on the other. Many design educators at this level have expressed their ill-disguised contempt at any suggestion that elementary or secondary school teachers could aspire to have anything to do with the serious teaching of design, other than as a form of arts appreciation. This attitude I believe to be still deeply entrenched and some significance may attach to it when those who are now critically interrogating the present progress of the movement turn their attention to the teachers themselves, rather than to the educands or the results of almost a decade of design education in the schools.

Other collaborators

Institutions of design represented by the professional design organisations and the promotional agencies established by the bureaucracies to encourage the design activity demonstrate a different form of intervention in the educational process.

Promotional agencies, similar to The Design Council (UK), now operate in many countries and especially where design is closely identifed with economic progress and development. We could believe they have played a significant role in shaping the general public's received view of the design activity and their continuing existence, in the political sense, depends on their demonstrable effectiveness in fulfilling this role.

All of them without exception have stressed the importance of design, 'good design', in the context of its contribution to economic success and the development of a healthy, technologically sophisticated and competitive manufacturing capability. They also provide supportive rhetoric for the promotion of the 'social significance' of design and its contribution to the improvement of the condition of mankind.

The flagship of this form of promotion has chiefly been the extolling of the virtues of consumer durables, the positional goods and services which have become, for most people in our society, the visible symbols of modernity, social mobility and economic progress.

It is true that some promotional agencies for design have recently changed their emphasis away from the consumer products which people acquire more from greed than need towards the large scale manifestation of the design process typified by intensive capital engineering products, urban and regional developments and the like. It is not clear whether this represents a more socially significant concern for the effects of design and planning, or the lack of it. Those who hold a cynical view of the design activity see this as another form of socialisation of the lay public towards the acceptance of the imperatives of a planned technological society. While I do not subscribe to such a pessimistic view of the work of these promotional organisations their traditional association with the highly instrumental and economic justifications for the significance of the design activity has provided some credibility and validity for the internal dissent among many educators engaged in teaching the visual and operational arts.

This particular view of the design process certainly formed little part of the original concept of design as education. The professional bodies representing the interests of the many kinds of design practitioners, while paying some attention to the socially significant aspects of design, need to be judged on their actual performance. Any review of the cultural inventory of our society expressed in terms of its products or product systems leads us to the conclusion that designers have so far contributed most of their energies to ensuring that their skills become indispensable to the entrepreneurial activities of those in command of the means of creating wealth in our society of conspicuous consumption.

Design: economic development and the illusion of modernity

It is not my place to comment upon the English or European scene in terms of assessing the contribution of design to achieving a better quality of life for its peoples and, more critically, of its direct contribution to the important solution of the problems of the growing inequalities and poverty of human living conditions. I do wish to reflect on what is now the case in my own adopted country, a country which has been vigorously promoted as the 'Lucky Country', Australia.

Australia is the most highly developed urban society in the world, perhaps the first such society but, in spite of its apparent sophistication, it is a highly under-developed country. It is fabulously rich in natural resources, possessed of a modern and highly diversified manufacturing and industrial technology, blessed by stable government and favoured, in the main, by an idyllic climate. One would anticipate that Australians, of all people, should have little cause for dissatisfaction with their way of life.

But Australians are also ill at ease. They too are trying to come to terms with the great paradox facing all advanced technological cultures, which is the non-fulfilment of the great eighteenth century European dream. That was the promise of the elimination of poverty, the building of a society of human grace and creative human possibilities through the emancipation of man from the struggle for physical survival which the inventions of science and the application of new technologies would bring.

Australia has never known the heel of an oppressor and never felt the trauma brought about by uncontrolled industrial development and its concomitant, the massive dislocations of urban renewal. It has also been able to learn from the errors of others. This it has done with some success even though Australia, as a vast new world, has never been exploited as the great living laboratory for creative human life experiment it is. Why then should Australians be so fearful about the future and why, in such a virgin place, should design intelligence have failed to make a greater contribution?

I believe that Australians, perhaps because of their 'Lucky Country' have also mistaken the outward materialistic trappings of their good life, most of which have been provided by the application of science, technology and economic imperatives, for the real thing.

Australians head the world in terms of proud ownership of their own homes, most of which sit on their own generous blocks of land. An explanation of the vast urban sprawl which is the real Australia is accounted for by this great preoccupation with the acquisition of that most prized of positional goods, a home of one's own. The great Australian dream is not in fact to have just one house, but two. The second being a beachside or bush retreat to get away from it all! Such an insatiable appetite for goods, possessions and property could only be met by the equivalent development of large scale service and communication systems. Such a profligate exploitation of available land also requires enormous investment in transportation systems but such as do exist, sophisticated as they may be, fail to operate efficiently or economically in face of the competition of the private automobile. Australians feel socially immobile, in all senses of that term, unless each household is at least a two car, even three car estab-lishment.

These systems for life are dominated by the anaesthetic international style of architecture, the predominant visual form of the cities on the one hand, and the sprawling obscenities of the manicured garden suburbs on the other. Australian domestic architecture typically is largely dominated by the bungalow, a sprawling confection of eclectic, often vulgar features, its useful human living spaces frequently subservient to the needs of housing and securing of the prime positional goods, the motor cars and not infrequently, the power boats and cabin cruisers that mark the successful Australian household more than any other symbol of modernity.

My own city of Perth situated as it is in a beautiful ocean and river setting recently celebrated the opening of yet another extension to its freeway system. This, together with a most elegantly conceived and brilliantly engineered bridge provides the most curious sensation of connecting one with a humanly sterile, monolithic city centre at one end and to a pot-pourri of indescribable human follies at the other. The journey between, at a mandatory 80 kilometres an hour, provides one with a kind of colour slide show, though necessarily brief, of the as yet unspoiled natural panorama of the beautiful Swan River. That is the face of progress and the illusion of modernity through design and economic development. No tears are shed for the destruction of natural environments and natural habitats which once boasted more than 7000 unique botanical species all of which were exquisitely designed to flourish in the equally unique climate of this beautiful country. The suburbs are rent with the noise of competing lawnmowers necessary to preserve the unnatural manicured lawns and vast sums are spent and precious natural water resources consumed each day in maintaining artificially contrived European gardens where before the natural flora and its fauna existed in healthy and vigorous profusion. Where then is 'design'? Australians live like fleas on the back of an animal they do not understand. Australia is a new country, but in that context so also will the vast regions of the so called under-developed countries become if the developers and economists have their way.

D.H. Lawrence writing about Australia during his visit in 1922 had this to say:

'You never knew anything so nothing ... as the life here. Australians are always vaguely on the go. That's what life in a new country does to you; it makes you so material, so outward, that your real inner life and your inner self dies out, and you clatter around like so many mechanical animals.'

And, some five decades later, another distinguished visitor and man of the arts, Sir Tyrone Guthrie, has this to say of my own fair city of Perth:

'A boring, materialistic quick-sand of sun-drenched steak fed vacuity'.

Therein, I suggest, lies the yet to be focused causes of the disquiet that ordinary Australians are now feeling in spite of the 'Lucky Country'. It is also, I suggest, the void that only the re-establishment of the visual and operational arts in education can hope to fill and that is why I share the concern of those who see the early constructive, co-operative initiatives of the Design in General Education Movement succumbing to the divisive and territorial claims of people who should know better. Perhaps Design with a capital 'D' was an unfortunate choice of descriptions.

Manners and customs

The old world, in spite of its savage mauling by the worst excesses of the industrial revolution, has still a sense of tradition through its careful preservation of its most historic towns and settlements, especially in Europe. I would be less than fair also not to recognise that some designers have made a contribution to the preservation of traditional ways of life, habits and customs in these places. Australia is now a multi-cultural society and most of its ethnic groupings derive from the old European world. One would have thought that something of these rich traditions and sense of identification that these people retain with their cultural and historic habitats may have informed the thinking and feeling of Australians about their land. I suspect that the economic imperatives, the rapacious greed for the products of economic development and the feeling that there was nothing 'man-made' to preserve in this unique and often dramatically beautiful 'wide brown land' has also dulled the sensitivities of these more recent settlers too. To be sure, Australians are not entirely the steak fed, self indulgent and materialistic morons portrayed by Guthrie and others. Indeed in pre-industrial, pre-economic days the early

settlers came to human terms with their wild and unpredictable new world, creating in the process habitats and artefacts almost as elegant as those of the true inheritors of the country, the aborigines. In this distinguished gathering the least said about the destruction of that magical culture the better.

Towards a new understanding of the human aesthetic design dimension

Dr Phil Roberts has recently re-examined the conventional practices of many arts, crafts, design and technology teachers who have been working within the framework of the new design in education initiatives and concludes:

'... The pointer is towards the need for a theory derived from the meanings of the underlying structure of the intentions, the happenings, the actions and the consequences that children (and adults) engage in when they are recognised as "designing". If that is so, it suggests a more appropriate model might consist in an evolutionary developmental model: a model grounded in action.'[1]

Here I suggest we have a direct connection being suggested with a potentially radical educational model. One which focuses upon ordinary human behaviours not just the behaviours identified with specific kinds of visual and operational arts educators or practitioners. Roberts, Baynes and others have also drawn attention to the domination of the specific exemplars of models of behaviour provided to children by the often opposing groups of practitioners which I briefly discussed earlier in this paper. The conclusion I sought to draw from this was that Fine Arts practitioners have become largely ineffectual, and tragically so, in reminding man of the biological necessity of engaging in these most important of human activities, while designers have allowed themselves to be anaesthetised by the politically expedient model of design as an economic necessity and a technological imperative. Where then is the middle ground to be found?

Since I believe the ground swell of interest in these critical educational developments has global implications let us consider a view of the design process or, more properly, the interrogative, creative, imaginative making and doing process, provided by yet another cultural insight.

Design as a cultural imperative

In discussing the theme of human action the distinguished Japanese designer Kenji Ekuan does not beat about the bush when it comes to stating the importance of the arts, crafts and design in general education.

'... To create "things" in arts and craft classes, at the planning level, pupils can study the theory of thought, and mathematical thoughts can be created too. Natural or social science and languages are similarly connected. Therefore arts and crafts should be made the main subject. Language and mathematics should be placed as minor subjects surrounding the arts. This means the change of the whole educational structure. If this is done, the unbalanced division of subjects will correspond to real life and there will be no children who dislike school.'[2]

And Ekuan again:

'If we give it a little thought, we will recognise that art and design education being closest to the "whole man" are most able to reflect total human activity. They are areas in which instinctive action, emotion and intelligence can act together.'[3]

Ekuan then draws closely upon the culturally given skills of learning respect for others, to provide an essentialist view of art and design education which relates to the social actions and consequences that children and adults engage in when they are creating or "designing":

'Here, besides learning how to make things, children should study their "manners" with products. When I use the word "manner" here, it has both the physical meaning, "how to use" and the social meaning of custom, "how to deal with". For example it is forbidden to make noise during dinner, or to close the door with the foot or various other manners of acting. I am not calling these manners to question here, but rather, I am questioning the social and cultural meaning of these conditions ... To join in the industrial society a position relative to "things" becomes a very important factor. I cannot help thinking that those characteristics like bad manners, arrogance, selfishness or deception are the factors that influence industry itself. I really hope that art and design education given to children will become the basis of excluding these violences of industrial society.'[4]

Design economics as a form of cultural intervention

If it is the case that man's social existence largely determines his consciousness then it seems obvious and necessary that design education, if it is to be tied to the concept of finding economic solutions to improving the quality of life, must also develop a methodology as well as a persuasive theoretical rhetoric. It must be seen *actually* to offer a better kind of social existence for all people than that which currently exists. So far I have suggested that design promotion has largely acted in our own society as a form of hallucinatory drug which supports the illusion of human progress through economic development.

Ideology, in order to be sustained, must be seen to have a meaning for the lived experience but this form of design ideology tied to the concept of planned economic and technological development or

modernity has chiefly addressed the solution of material problems. That is of course if one believes that designers, acting as satraps of our dominant entrepreneurial economic society, are actually addressing real human needs.

We are prepared to question the contributions made to date by design in such advanced societies as England, Europe and the United States where, we believe, ordinary people have some understanding and therefore control over the forces which determine how they should live. How then will we be able to avoid the repetition of the distortions and misrepresentations of the nature of the design acitivity in those vast, poverty-stricken, under-developed countries which, alas, also aspire to the same conditions of modernity we presently enjoy?

Most of these under-developed nations have a great potential for economic development: why else are our economists and technocrats so interested in them? They are also societies of great complexity and enormous social inequalities. Because of the historical neglect of the most basic forms of education they are also handicapped by a widespread collective, submissive consciousness.

In the company of so many distinguished designers and educators from these places, who are attending and making contributions to this conference, I acknowledge that they are doing a great deal of careful thinking about the introduction of design as an important strategy in overcoming many deeply distressing human problems. I beg their indulgence if I now take an example of the kind of design intervention which, I believe, is misdirected in this absolutely critical area of concern.

A possible exemplar being set for the promotion of the activity of design as a strategy central to the economic development and modernisation of under-developed countries may be deduced from the outcomes of the recent ICSID/UNIDO/India Conference held in January, 1979, at Ahmedabad in India, which led subsequently to the widely acclaimed Ahmedabad Declaration on Design for Development.

I have no intention of taking issue with many of the very sensible and constructive recommendations contained within that Declaration. What I do take issue with is the fundamental assumption made in it that 'engaging in' the design activity is almost totally grounded in the view that design must be set in the context of building a large manufacturing capability. Thus, it is posited, will the quality of life for the great masses of people living in the Indian sub-continent be dramatically improved.

The implications of this form of design promotion and design consciousness-raising are just as relevant to our understanding and solving of the current social and economic crisis of Western advanced societies as they are to the people to whom they are directed. Such statements imply that Design with a capital 'D' has helped to achieve those things which have made technology not only desirable in economic terms, but also in terms of its response to meeting deeply human needs and aspirations.

Secure and self-confident in the illusion of the appropriateness of the design and technology model and that equation most promoted by the technocrats, production = efficiency = economic and social success, the supportive rhetoric of this Declaration made little direct reference to the critical infrastructures of marketing, promotion, advertising and all the supporting consumer-oriented industries so central to a manufacturing economy and society of conspicuous consumption. They may have been subsumed under the several references to the need to 'communicate' about design.

A note of dissent

One address, given as a keynote contribution to the India Conference, thankfully reminds us that Indians do respect and love the rich cultural heritage of their immediate and distant past and are not likely to be so easily hoodwinked by the promotors of design as economics so quickly. In an address, which received wide media coverage Mr. Thapar suggested that:

'Designers had a central role in creating an Indian national identity by linking inherited aesthetics and contemporary needs. A crisis of identity was prevalent throughout the Third World and was expressed in *dangerous imitations*. A wave of vulgarity was sweeping India and other nations. In India the battle was far from won because vulgarity in all its frustrations, its duplicity and imitation has the propensity to return with redoubled fury.'

This coupling of the notion of vulgarity with that of frustration, duplicity and imitation is, I suggest, a telling comment. It relates to the underlying frustrations of most people in our own society who have been so long exposed to the 'benefits' of the consumer-driven manufacturing industries and the bureaucratic interventions of the planners, economists and technocrats.

People do not only need to obtain things, goods, services and utilities. They desperately need to have some sense of autonomy and responsibility as well as the opportunity to influence and to make decisions about how they live, and what kinds of goods and services they need as well as some sense of the relationship of these things to the welfare of the community as a whole.

Ekuan's analogy of design intelligence with culturally given manners or ways of behaving relates to this and provides perhaps the true essence of the way in which design in education was intended to develop.

This is also another way of saying that the arts and design in education have the obligation to take these fully human, aesthetic, creative practices back into a sick society. Clearly a re-examination of all that is good in the conventional practices of our visual and operational arts educators should be made, as Roberts and Baynes have said, without isolating these within the narrow, prescriptive boundaries of subject areas and specialisms.

Design education and the developing countries

This conference predictably provides an encyclopaedic coverage of design activities but I believe that none of the high sounding and no doubt useful and interesting topics will be of any real or lasting value unless there is a clear understanding of what Design in General Education is all about. The critical focus of these activities in our elementary and secondary schools must be identified as a fundamental and central aspect of creative and mental growth. Arts education in our Western world has gone badly wrong. The human need and capacity for creative work should develop as a continuum from the spontaneous, individualised creative exploration of the young child into the meaningful, purposeful, creative but fully social inventions and interventions of the adult. The attitudes of mind we should be seeking to develop cannot be achieved through institutionalising the perfectly valid behaviour of the inquisitive infant artists as an adult activity, as has occurred in the Fine Arts, or by imposing the highly instrumental and anaesthetic values of design for extrinsic economic or technological purposes as in vocationally oriented Design. It can only be achieved through each person's mastery of acting creatively upon the world. That is by the making of art, and making of artefacts informed by and informing the developing, contextual, cultural and social growth of every person.

Educators who have already contributed so much to the development of the creative arts in early and secondary education and especially those who have been engaged in the Design in General Education Movement must understand that the developing countries of the world may well look to them for such guidance and inspiration. The all too facile and politically respectable promotion of design in an economic context is a model that will find an all too enthusiastic acceptance in these places. Most of the forms of education given priority as symbols of development and modernity are those which promise to make immediate contributions to the ubiquitous GNP. Let us be mindful of the socially and culturally disintegrative effects of exporting our educational strategies which we know to be imperfectly developed. We need of course, to get our own arts, crafts, design and technology education right, where it matters most, in early and general education.

May I also suggest that unless we wish to see our errors compounded on a global scale, urgent attention should be given now to developing exchanges of information with all those people currently engaged in international educational development work, especially in the elementary and secondary school sectors. Perhaps this conference might usefully adopt, as part of its recommendations on Design Policy for World Futures, that UNESCO and other related international agencies for the advancement of education and cultural affairs encourage such educational developments as a matter of some urgency.

It is so difficult for deprived societies to resist the exponential growth of technology and the promise of modernity and economic well-being it will bring when people do not have a roof over their heads, a source of power, of water, of nutritious food and basic health care. Of course the developing countries must create sensible opportunities and facilities for educating designers at the professional level alongside the established provisions for engineering, science, medicine, and in the context of their own social, cultural and development programmes. What I am suggesting is that these places do have an opportunity to introduce these things in beginning education and thus avoid the tyranny of the received view of the art and design and technological activity imposed on our elementary and secondary education from above. They have the chance to learn from our errors as well as our achievements and we should help them to do this in the interests of building a better world.

References

1   Roberts, Phil, *Why might Art Teachers and Craft Teachers, in particular, have been looking critically at their conventional practices*, Design Education Unit, Royal College of Art, 1981.
2   Ekuan, Kenji, *Ekuan, Dunhill Industrial Design Australian Lectures 1973*, Industrial Design Council of Australia, Trevor Wilson, p 53.
3   *Ibid*.
4   *Ibid*.
5   ICSID *Executive Board Report 1977–79 Brussels,* pp 47–49.

Design for low-income economies

Professor Nathan H. Shapira, IDSA
Department of Art, Design and Art History, University of California, Los Angeles

To contribute effectively to economic development, designers in low-income economies need to become familiar with problems related to limited purchasing power, appropriate technologies, recycling, industrial development, economic planning and multiple cultural frameworks. An educational programme should equip them with the multi-disciplinary awareness necessary to balance conflicting pressures created by the acceleration of mass production, distribution and consumption.

The graduate seminar on 'Design for Low-Income Economies' started in 1975 at the University of California Los Angeles, and consisted of a team of teachers acting as facilitators, students doing original research and visiting professionals sharing their knowledge and experience. Seminar topics include shelter, health, education, rural development, urbanisation, and the significant role of cultural heritage. This paper discusses the general nature of the seminar and concludes with a presentation of some of the projects which it has spawned. Among them are visual identity programmes, primary health care kits, mobile markets, and furniture systems.

The seminar of graduate studies in Industrial Design on 'Design for Low-Income Economies', open also to students in Architecture and Urban Planning, was started in the Department of Art, Design and Art History of the University of California, Los Angeles in 1975. Its aims are to familiarise students with the expanded socio-economic role of the designer in developing countries and to prepare the background for competent professional problem-solving activities. The seminar, defined as: 'a course of study pursued by a group of advanced students doing original research under a professor',[1] is considered to be an informational community with the instructor acting as a facilitator rather than a fountain of knowledge, students processing information and visitors sharing their experiences and research. In his Japan Prize lecture, Wilbur Schramm pointed out that a new role for the teacher and individualised instruction are the main currents in modern education:

'... the teacher is coming to be a kind of stage manager for a number of learning activities – television, films, books, programmed instruction, explanation, discussion, practice, experiments, individual projects, field trips and many others. The focus has moved from the teacher teaching to the student learning: the teacher's job is to arrange a series of learning opportunities that will fit the individual student's needs and capabilities and stimulate him to learn in the only way he can learn in his own way, at his own rate, by his own efforts ....'[2]

The duration of the seminar is limited to one 12-week term. Group meetings take place once a week for three hours, while tutorial individual meetings frequently take place as needed. The content and the various topics discussed at the seminar are based on the belief that no specific aspect of design can be considered outside a multi-disciplinary context. The topics discussed cover diverse traditional frameworks, limited purchasing power, survival priorities, use of local resources and appropriate technologies, recycling, social transformation, industrial development and economic planning. Visiting experts share their experiences in the fields of shelter, education, health, politics, rural development and technical co-operation. Some of the discussions are related to assigned readings; among the recommended texts are Denis Goulet's *The Uncertain Promise*,[3] Paul W. DeVore's *An Introduction to Technology*,[4] Lester Brown's *World Without Borders*,[5] and David Dickson's *Alternative Technology*.[6]

At the beginning of each term, students choose a project related to their interests and carry it out individually or in teams. Occasionally these projects become the initial stage of a thesis for a graduate degree. Such theses take from six to twelve months to complete. They are supervised by a thesis committee comprising at least three members of the regular design staff. Students may also invite outside consultants to participate in the meetings of the committee. When completed, graduate theses are displayed in the University's Frederick S. Wright Art Gallery as part of the Annual Graduate Students Exhibition which is open to the public for three to four weeks. Whether or not a student project becomes a thesis, from time to time it is presented at the end of the term as a printed paper, while the presentations made in class are summarised and published in a newspaper format.

Figure 1.
A modular house for affordable living.

A diverse number of products were started or developed in this seminar. Some projects, such as the visual identity programmes, the portable primary health care kit, the mobile market and the working station, became graduate theses; others, like the knock-down shelving system, the containing partitions, the children's furniture, the recycled tin cans used for walking in snow, and the second use for pvc pipes, were developed in upper-division undergraduate courses; finally the modular house for affordable living (Figure 1) is currently in the development stage and scheduled for completion in the near future.

Five graduate theses

The following accounts of graduate theses came out of the seminar and each suggests a design solution for specific needs of low-income economies.

Two visual identity programmes

The movement toward political independence in the low-income economies has intensified the need for industrialisation and expanded trade; at the same time the urbanisation process has accelerated beyond the pace of the industrialised nations. The importance of a visual identity programme is even greater in low-income economies than in industrialised nations because of their higher level of illiteracy and their greater variety of languages. These communication barriers can be overcome with the aid of effective 'visual identity programmes'. In addition to the private sector, the public sector and the para-statal organisations are all participating in a wide process of shaping new cultural identities. A 'visual identity programme' is a unified plan covering the design of all visual elements related to a certain organisation or commercial enterprise. The purpose of such a programme is to insure that each visual element facilitates identification and projects an image which reinforces the viewer's awareness of that particular organisation. Allan W. Green has developed a thesis project along these lines from a seminar assignment related to the visual identity programmes of Zambia's Red Cross Society and Kenya's New Era periodical. The study for the Zambia Red Cross Society led to the development of a manual for the visual identity programme. The purpose of this manual was to enable the administrative personnel of the Society to make design decisions related to such needs as stationery, forms, posters, announcements, invitations, bulletins, newsletters, annual reports, displays, architectural signage, vehicle identification, uniforms, badges, package and interiors. Univers medium 65 type-face caps were selected for the logo of the Society, while Univers 55 light and Univers 75 bold in upper and lower-case were selected for texts and publicity because of their high legibility, clean appearance and local availability. Because some of

the posters and announcements are addressed to pre-literate groups in the rural areas, specific recommendations were developed to support an awareness for a diversity of local customs and traditional values.

The architectural signage comprising identification signs and directional signs emphasised the need for simplicity to maximise the clarity of the messages.

A multi-purpose visual matrix inspired by a traditional basket-weaving pattern was developed for a diversity of uses, such as window curtains, wallpapers, lampshades, wrapping paper, paper bags, greeting cards, blouses and head-dresses for volunteers and nurses (Figures 2 and 3); sections of various sizes of these matrices could be easily selected by administrative staff without design background for urgent two-dimensional visual decisions.

Figures 2 and 3.
Visual identity programme for the Zambia Red Cross Society, inspired by a traditional basket weaving design.

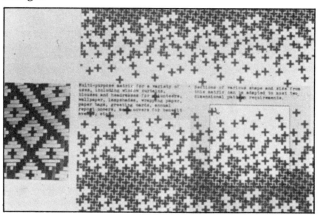

The logo for the New Era magazine published in Kenya for high school pupils was inspired by a traditional African stool; it was conceived for repetitive use. The pattern obtained by repeating the logo has numerous applications in fabrics used as curtains, table covers, wall covers, and so on.

Portable primary health care kit

The objective of mobile health care system in low-income economies is the improvement of the general health level of the population by treatment of the sick, prevention of disease, and health education. Health education plays an important role because it makes both the prevention and treatment of disease more effective. The health level of any group of people depends more on the availability of good primary health care than on advanced hospitals. With the encouragement of the World Health Organisation many governments, especially in the newly independent countries, are giving high priority to the development of an efficient primary health service which is more efficient and more economical than the traditional development of a highly advanced network of hospitals. A primary health care service depends on the mobile health clinic and the mobility of the medical care worker. Usually its priorities are concerned with temporary bed care, ambulatory, extended care on-site, physiotherapy, dental aid, excreta disposal, water supply improvement, family planning, food protection, nutrition, spray techniques against insects, health education for the general public, and the administration of medical records. Frequently the medical practitioner has to travel to remote areas to administer routine medical treatment, check-ups or innoculation for diseases. This situation is created either by the lack of medical facilities in these areas or because of the nomadic conditions of migratory workers or traditional cultural groups. A mobile health care unit could be transported to a

Figure 4.
Portable primary health storage kit.

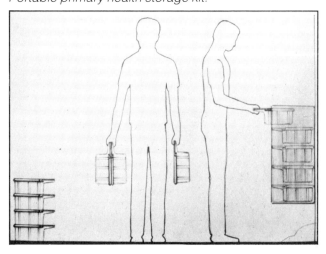

Figure 5.
Portable health kit with shoulder strap.

remote site to establish a temporary medical station. The basic component of a mobile health care system consists of a paramedic with minimal equipment being carried to a remote area. The paramedic's function may be to do a specific disease-oriented survey or an assignment to innoculate the members of a rural community against infectious diseases. In addition to his assignment the paramedic would give attention to medical problems related to his expertise. Paramedics might be attached to a fixed health or to a mobile health facility. Transportation can be a very difficult problem to overcome due to road conditions or the limitation of means which can include vans, motorcycles, airplanes, or camels.

The thesis of Ricardo Gomez had two objectives:

a   the development of a mobile health care unit (mini-trailer);
b   the development of a hand-carried, portable primary health storage kit to be used either as a shelving unit in a modular compartment of a mobile health care trailer (Figure 4), or as a hand-carried primary health kit to be used on field trips.

The mini-trailer was made with modular corrugated bent aluminum panels (2' wide), which slide lock together on a steel finger joint core. A cast aluminum alloy base and roof reinforced the structure. The dimensions of the mini-trailer are 10' × 7' × 6'. The primary health portable kit was to be for a wide range of uses, from a midwife's kit to a file for medical records (a function which could be fulfilled because of its stacking capabilities). The interior trays of the portable kit are interlocking and removable to accommodate a variety of irregular sizes; they may slide in vertically or horizontally. The cover slides and locks the case; it can be used as a writing or working surface.

The portable kit is built of durable injection moulded pvc plastic and can be used for storage of supplies, instruments and medication, for records and sterilisation; also as a water container; for a work surface, seating, working and writing; when placed cover to cover, two containers could be easily carried together. A shoulder strap can be attached to facilitate portability (Figure 5).

Mobile markets in Mexico City

Mexico City, with 14 million people, is one of the fastest growing cities; demographic forecasts indicate that it will be the most populous city by the beginning of the next millennium.

Among many other urgent priorities, the government and private sector are concerned with the commercial problems related to an increased distribution system of consumer goods to a constantly expanding population. In addition to markets and supermarkets, to department stores and speciality stores, small stores, and street vendors, there is a traditional market that dates from Pre-Colombian times as represented in a display from the National Archeological Museum and that still survives in an adapted form today. These traditional markets are the *tianguis* or *mercados sobre ruedas*, better known as *mobile markets*. The main objective of these markets is to take hard-to-find merchandise to various areas of the city. The cycle starts when the merchant is buying his product in the central supply market. Once the items are purchased, they are loaded in a small truck to be transported to the many sectors of the city, where temporary displays are set up to entice the prospective buyers. At the end of the day, the unsold merchandise is packed and loaded in the truck which soon will be lost in the heavy traffic of the city until the next day, when the cycle starts all over again. Bernardo Baran's study started with extensive field surveys in Mexico City; a comparative photographic investigation of several *tianguis* indicated the location of these markets and some of the urgent design needs. The basic idea was to develop a system of components, easy to manufacture with local materials and technologies. By producing a large quantity of these standardised elements, their cost could be low and the municipality could make them available to the entire city. A sense of visual coherence easily identifiable will attract consumers and create an environment that will enhance the city.

To date most of the *tianguis*, as revealed by Baran's photographic survey, need improvements. Some of them are using old inadequate buildings; others are very primitive using the street's floor for display with an occasional umbrella to protect the vendor against the sun.

In most cases the merchandise and the consumers are not protected. The current trend is to use fabrics with a wooden or metal structure to create a shaded environment, but the structures are not standardised nor conceived as modular systems. Storage and signage are other areas which need improvement. Since the *tianguis* offer a variety of items, from edibles to clothes and containers such as baskets, pots, metal and plastic brackets, consumers in the market frequently have a hard time locating what they need.

Considering all the need areas revealed by field studies and photographic surveys in Mexico City, the solution proposes a modular system of foldable tables equipped with two large colour-coded umbrellas and stacking standard plastic containers (Figure 6). All components of this system are foldable and easily transported by relatively small vehicles. A signage system offers much flexibility; its elements are well integrated into the rest of the system.

Modular working stations

This project, conceived for Brazil, involves a large-scale production in plywood, a commodity abundantly available there. The simplicity of the standard components requires a minimum investment for tooling in the manufacturing process. The assembly of the standard components can be accomplished by unskilled labour with minimal basic tools, such as screwdrivers and pliers.

Figure 6.
Model of a portable stall system for mobile markets in Mexico City.

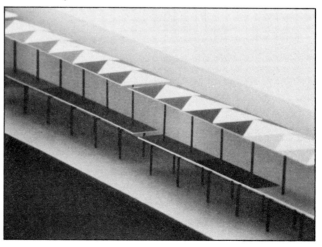

This modular system is not limited to a specific product; instead it is conceived as a language that can solve a variety of needs; in addition to office interiors it can be used in libraries, hospitals, schools, store-rooms, restaurants, shops, etc. This study of Sergio de Andrade focuses on three basic elements: storage, working spaces and partitions (Figure 7). The system combines a commercially available metal fastener and polypropylene caps with specially produced steel cylindrical connectors and standardised 3/4″ plywood panels (Figure 8). The cylinders have eight lateral perforations connecting to the panels and a longitudinal perforation to house, when necessary, electrical wires, or to attach to casters or other accessories. All these elements are connected by a system called the Knock Down Fitting Spannfix. The edge of the panel is curved by a machining process using a specially adapted blade. The dimensions of the panels are standardised to 91 sizes obtained from a basic 12″ × 12″ module. Holes to receive connectors are drilled following a standard grid.

The dimensions of the assembled units are related to human factors, to the functional requirements of the working process and to various sizes of office and drafting supplies, materials, instruments and equipment. Standard commercially available accessories such as trays and casters can be inserted into the system.

A modular house for affordable living

This house is part of a project which may be developed for the 1987 UN International Year of Shelter for the Homeless. It was started with a small grant from the UCLA Academic Senate Research Committee in 1978 by Professor Christopher Williams and a group of design students; it aims to offer an affordable home for low-income groups, easy to ship and simple to assemble. The building is based on standard hollow panels 4″ thick obtained from two particle board panels 4′ × 8′ × 4″ locked with a 3″ × 4″ lumber framework. All components are pre-manufactured and assembled with unskilled labour on site. This house intended for a family with two children has three bedrooms, two baths, living and dining areas and kitchen; its total area is about 1400 sq feet and its costs amounts to approximately $10 per square foot. The roof configuration is adapted to the use of solar energy equipment (Figure 1).

Conclusion

A natural conclusion of this presentation would be the search for future directions on the bases of the results and experiences acquired in this seminar. Obviously the directions will depend on the future trends of our educational system, which has been struggling in recent years with a no-growth situation or, in our administrative language, is in a 'steady state'.

Figure 7.
Modular working stations are divided into three basic elements: storage, working spaces and partitions.

Figure 8.
The joining system of the working station comprises a specially produced steel cylindrical connector and two commercially produced metal fasteners with two polypropylene caps.

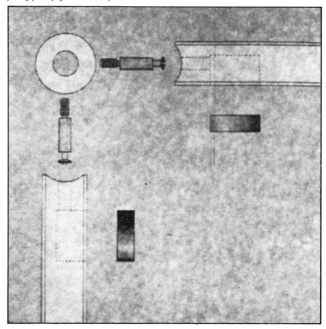

One desirable development would be to expand the scope of the seminars to include poverty areas of the industrialised economies as well as low-income economies.

Since our students usually come either from low-income economies or are interested in a professional career in the industrial development field, it seems advisable to structure the entire programme around projects related to research for real needs and situations. This clinical education approach structured around studio and laboratory work cannot be carried out without a minimum multi-disciplinary theoretical background covering elementary aspects of management, economics, rural and industrial development, education, social and political sciences, health and cultural traditions.

Such design programmes can be implemented most effectively if they are established in university environments where they can benefit from the richness of the available multi-disciplinary resources.

References

1   Merriam, G.C. *The New Merriam Webster Dictionary*, New York, 1971.
2   Armsey, W. James, Dahl, C. Norman, *An Inquiry into the Uses of Instructional Technology*, The Ford Foundation, New York, 1973.
3   Goulet, Denis, *The Uncertain Promise*, Overseas Development Council, Washington DC, 1975.
4   DeVore, Paul W., *An Introduction to Technology*, Davis Publications, Worcester, Massachusetts, 1980.
5   Brown, Lester, *World Without Borders*, Random House, New York, 1975.
6   Dickson, David, *Alternative Technology*, Fontana – Collins, London, 1974.

Simple design-and-build projects as an aid in teaching engineering design

A.E. Churches
Senior Lecturer, School of Mechanical and Industrial Engineering, University of New South Wales, Australia

Design-and-build projects may be a useful means of increasing students' design experience, particularly in the creative and practical aspects, during the early years of their course. Such projects help students to realise that several different solutions may be viable, that simple calculations may provide useful design data, and that simple design brings its own rewards in easy construction and efficient performance.

Introduction

Teachers of mechanical engineering design often face a dilemma in trying to blend creativity, theory and practice within the restrictions of an undergraduate course, particularly in the earlier years.

Theoretical aspects cause little difficulty, since they are well covered in a variety of textbooks. Nevertheless, even here some hard choices may be necessary when 'important' sections of the work cannot be fitted into the available time. It may then become a matter of covering fewer topics more thoroughly.

It has probably been the experience of many engineering design lecturers that numerous practical problems, having a 'real engineering' flavour, can be found without difficulty. Indeed, lecturers usually seem to have a stock of such problems arising from their own industrial experience. The difficulty here is that there can be no rational solution without an adequate understanding of the background – the so-called 'feel' for the project – and such understanding is acquired only through extensive experience in that particular industry. The lecturer is thus left with the almost impossible task of conveying this experience, or background, to the student within the confines of a student exercise. By the time such problems are presented to the students, after being disentangled from their industrial context and reduced to a scope suitable for the early years of an undergraduate course, there may be little of the real engineering flavour remaining.

Other difficulties may arise in setting creative design assignments. First, particularly in the early part of their course, students have little theory at their disposal and may find it difficult to carry their design much beyond the creative stage. Secondly, there may be pitfalls in formulating the creative assignments. On the one hand, the problem may eventually be recognised as trivial; on the other hand, it may become so large and complex that it is more suited to a consultant consortium than an undergraduate. Other problems may prove to be so worked over that it is almost impossible to devise novel solutions.

As an example of the difficulties which may arise, creative design assignments have been set as a major part of the first year Engineering Design course at the University of New South Wales for the past 15 or more years.[1] During that time, the type of creative assignment has gradually been forced to change as more and more topic areas have been covered by review type articles appearing in the popular science press, leaving little scope for further creative thinking. Hence a typical assignment in the first year is now more likely to be 'find a means of preventing washing from getting wet in a sudden shower', rather than the earlier type, which often addressed larger scale problems: 'Suggest a system or method whereby copious supplies of fresh water can be made available to the Barren Island Republic'.

In these projects, students concentrate on creative thinking followed by some elementary decision making, but little detailed analysis is expected. First year students generally find that such a project provides a rewarding design experience. However, by the middle of the second year a different format is appropriate.

Second year Mechanical Design at the University of New South Wales is devoted to a study of the effects of material properties and manufacturing methods on the design process. Regular assignments involve the design of simple machine elements. The year culminates in the design of a complete machine, typically having a motor, belt drive, housing, shaft and bearings, seals, and so on. Although care is taken to avoid 'handbook' design as much as possible, it would be easy, in such a programme, to forget the importance of creativity in engineering design. The design-and-build project in the second year is seen as complementing the machine design projects, since it requires the application of creative thinking, followed by the more practical aspects of construction, modification (or redesign) and testing. Actually building and testing the proposed design allows the students to carry the design process several steps further than a normal theoretical exercise.

Project requirements

Perhaps the most important requirement for a successful design-and-build project is that there be several different solution types or concepts, each offering a feasible alternative. A project in which all students chose the same basic concept would be regarded as less than successful. As an aid to creative thinking, the problem is described in general terms of what is to be achieved, rather than how the task is to be performed. For example, in one recent project the students were asked to devise a means of lifting as much water as possible to a higher level in a given time, using only two students to provide the input power.

The word 'pump' does not appear in the problem formulation and, as may be seen from Appendix A, the students chose a wide range of solutions or concepts, ranging from piston type pumps of various configurations, through peristaltic, diaphragm and bellows pumps to bucket chains and even single buckets.

Ideally, there should not be an existing solution to the problem posed. If a solution does already exist, as in the case of the problem cited above, it can often be ruled out on the grounds of cost or by careful manipulation of the problem restrictions, eg all items to be purchased from a suburban hardware store, not from a specialist engineering supplier.

The need for students to construct their proposed designs imposes one of the major restrictions on the type of project which can be set. Many students do not have access to a wide range of tools and equipment and it is impracticable for the school to provide access to machine tools. Hence, to be equitable, all construction is restricted to the use of hand tools, and no welding or brazing is permitted.

As well as material availability, material costs need to be considered. Students are expected to purchase their own materials, hence the projects need to be constrained so that some students are not at a disadvantage compared with their more affluent peers.

As examples of typical design-and-build projects, brief summaries of several projects which have been used are collected in Appendix A, and a somewhat condensed version of the handout sheet for Project WET (the water-lifting task cited earlier) appears as Appendix B.

Figure 1.
Design-and-build project: crossing water quickly without getting wet.

Project organisation

A period of four weeks is usually allowed between issuing the project specification and the final testing. However, the normal machine element design programme continues during this period and only the final testing is held in class time. The design-and-build project usually carries approximately 10% of the total marks for the subject.

Students work in groups of three or four. At the end of the first two weeks, each group is required to submit a preliminary report specifying the group's chosen concept. At this stage, it is usually possible to gauge the success of the project, to clear up any misconceptions and to make minor changes to the rules, should this be necessary.

Simple order-of-magnitude calculations are encouraged and can frequently be used to show whether or not certain types of solution are feasible. Class tutors provide guidance with the analysis if requested, but do not suggest possible solutions.

The completed devices are required to be handed in 24 hours before the final testing. A panel of judges then assesses creativity and quality of construction, giving each a mark between one and ten. Students provide details of cost, assuming all material was new and was purchased on the basis of the smallest commercially available quantity. In some projects, the weight or size may need to be recorded for assessment purposes.

Where considered appropriate, students are required to submit a prediction of their device's performance level prior to final testing.

The final testing of students' devices is the high point of the project, and probably the high point of the year's work. The University of New South Wales holds a biennial Open Day and in these years testing is timed to coincide with Open Day. In the alternate years, testing is still organised as a public event, usually in a prominent location, and staff and students from other years are encouraged to attend. The device which performs best over the day's testing receives full marks for performance, while the worst performance is allotted 10% or 15%. Devices which fail during the day's testing score zero.

Final reports are due one week after testing. The reports are required to list the solutions considered, to state the reasons for choosing the adopted solution and to show any mathematical analysis used. The predicted and actual performance levels should be compared, and reasons given for any discrepancy.

A critical appraisal of the chosen design is an important feature of the report and frequently serves to emphasise the benefits to be gained from greater attention to creative thinking and the use of some simple calculations.

Discussion

There appears to be little published information on design projects of the design-and-build type in undergraduate engineering courses.[2,3,4] While the University of Utah has featured prominently in these publications, it is not clear whether design-and-build projects are a regular part of their undergraduate courses. The University of Wollongong (NSW, Australia)[2,5] uses creative design projects as the major part of the first year Engineering Design curriculum. Students choose one of several creative topics offered and are encouraged to build a working model if possible. Final assessment is by a panel of judges rather than a competition to determine the best performance. However, it seems probable that the design-and-build projects of similar format are being used at many other colleges and universities throughout the world, and one of the purposes of this paper is to promote discussion and the exchange of ideas in the general teaching area.

The design-and-build projects set so far at the University of New South Wales, summarised in Appendix A, were felt to be worthwhile design experiences for the students. Working in groups of four, even the most inexperienced student group has always managed to devise some sort of solution to the problem set. There have been occasions when a group's submission has obviously been badly prepared, perhaps completely untested, but such examples have been rare and the students involved have readily admitted that the fault lay in lack of effort on their part.

One of the major benefits of a successful design-and-build project is the demonstration that there may be more than one viable solution to a problem. Students sometimes comment after the event that they became fixed on a particular concept which was suggested by a group member, and made no real effort in creative thinking. The fact that not all possible solutions are equally efficient in a given application is also demonstrated, as students watch the performance of different designs. It may, however, be necessary to point out how design details and quality of construction affect the various designs and their performance. In this context, it would become evident that simple, elegant design brings its own rewards in easy construction and effective performance.

Students are often gratified to find that their meagre knowledge of theory may nevertheless provide useful design data. For example, in the water pumping project, a first estimate of the optimum size of a piston pump may be found from the hydrostatic pressure and the piston area. The basic error of one group, who turned up at the final testing with an (untested) two cylinder piston pump of some 250mm diameter to raise water through a height of three metres, was quickly recognised by several other groups.

Occasionally, minor difficulties have been experienced in running the projects. It has sometimes been necessary to make last-minute changes to the rules to clarify the acceptability or rejection of certain classes of solution which were not anticipated in the original problem formulation. Such changes, no matter how carefully done, always seem to cause some dissatisfaction and should be avoided, if at all possible, by careful phrasing of the original problem definition. Questions related to material cost have caused more difficulties than any other aspect. Some students always manage to find heavily discounted items or offcuts of 'new' material sold at give-away prices. Nevertheless, it is felt that cost is such an important factor that it should be included wherever possible in an engineering design problem.

The projects set so far have been confined to mechanical contrivances, with only simple mechanisms and mechanical-to-mechanical energy conversion. Projects involving the mechanical conversion of heat have been avoided, since such projects demand very well made, mechanically efficient devices and may not work at all if this criterion cannot be met. Even so, it has been obvious in several projects that minimisation of frictional losses has been the major design criterion – a condition which occurs not infrequently in real-life engineering design.

It has been the experience of all staff members involved with the class that student interest increases and that there is an improved class spirit, possibly because students and staff have had the opportunity of working closely together on another type of design problem. Students often comment that they enjoyed the project and felt they benefited from it, with the need to build, modify and rebuild their proposed design adding significantly to their design experience. Some students ask whether another design-and-build project could be organised later in the year. However, the curriculum is already crowded, the preparation and setting up of projects requires a significant time, and it seems likely that fewer benefits would be derived from a second project. Accordingly, it is intended to continue the use of design-and-build projects in the way they are now being used – as an occasional aid and high point in teaching the creative and practical aspects of engineering design.

Acknowledgements

The design-and-build projects could not have been run without the contributions and assistance of all members of the Design Group. The idea of such projects was originally introduced at the University of New South Wales by Professor N.L. Svensson, at that time Head of the Department of Applied Mechanics.

References

1   Svensson, N.L. *Introduction to Engineering Design* 2nd ed New South Wales University Press, Kensington, NSW, 1981, p 119.

2   Student Design Contest – 'Engineers are Slipping at the University of Utah' and 'Motivation is the Goal in Australian Competition', *Machine Design,* Vol 46 July 25, 1974, p 20.
3   'A Short Course in Carpet Climbing', *Machine Design,* Vol 48 Oct 7, 1976, p 35.
4   'Screen Test for Le Mouse II', *Machine Design,* Vol 49 Jan 20, 1977, p 22.
5   Wheway, R.T. 'Motivation via Creative Design', *The Journal of the Institution of Engineers, Australia.* Vol 43 No 6, June 1971, p 9.

Appendix A
Summary of some design-and-build projects

Project name	Task	Concepts used	Comments
RUBICON	Find a means of crossing a given stream without getting wet. All equipment to fit into garbage can. Minimum time criterion.	Bridges – truss – plank (in sections) Canoe (made from garbage cans). Raft (plastic bags). Wet suit and snorkel tube.	Rapid assembly and set up was the key to this project. Plank type bridges performed best.
FLINTSTONE	Build a vehicle to carry 2 students over a specified course, using no metal in the construction. Vehicle to be propelled without students touching the ground.	Tricycle, double bicycle, billy cart. Propulsion by pedals, levers, 'oars'.	Very successful and spectacular event. Several mechanical failures during the event. Several different designs were equally viable.
PEP (Potential Energy Propulsion)	Transfer potential energy from a falling weight to a vehicle and store the energy in the vehicle. Use the stored energy to drive the vehicle as far as possible.	Energy generally stored in springs although some used gravitational potential energy and one used a flywheel. Wide variety of springs used. Vehicles of 2, 3 and 4 wheel construction.	Rapid acceleration types were not successful. Flywheel was unsuccessful. Two wheel vehicle with gravitational PE was the winner. Friction was the major obstacle to be overcome.
WET (Water Elevation and Transportation)	Raise as much water as possible through a height of 3m in 1 minute using 2 students as source of power.	Piston pumps of various designs – 1 and 2 cylinder single and double acting. Peristaltic, bellows and diaphragm pumps. Bucket chain, single bucket. Telescoping concentric cylinders.	While cylinder type pumps were by far the most popular, there were sufficient concepts to make the project highly successful. Telescoping concentric cylinder pump was the most successful.
MATCH (Mechanical Arrangement of the Traditional game of Chuck Ha'penny	Design a mechanical coin tossing machine to match the performance of those who have more time to practise than engineering students.	Not yet available. (To be run in 1982.)	This is somewhat of a new venture, requiring a machine to give accurate and reproducible results.

Appendix B

The University of New South Wales
School of Mechanical and Industrial Engineering
5.122 Mechanical Design
Design and Build Project 1981
Project WET (Water Elevation and Transportation)

Introduction: The aim of a design-and-build project is to give you the opportunity of taking your design beyond the drawing board stage to see how your ideas actually work out in practice. Also, in the preliminary stages of testing the device you have constructed, you are able to modify and develop your design to improve its performance. These are extremely important stages in the learning process of the designer as they help him or her to develop a feeling for what will or will not work in practice.

In this year's project you will work in groups of four (4) to design and construct a man-powered device for lifting water from one level to a higher level. This is a common problem in the irrigation of farmland and in the less developed countries is often carried out very inefficiently by the use of buckets or crudely constructed lifting devices. The aim of this project is to show how the problem might be solved more effectively using readily available materials, simple hand tools and the creative minds of young engineers. You have four weeks to complete the project.

Objective: To construct a man-powered device which will lift as much water as possible through a height of 3 metres in a period of one minute. The device may be operated by one or two persons.

Test set-up: The devices which you construct will be tested on the University Open Day. The layout of the test facility is shown on a separate sheet. However, to allow you to test your device prior to Open Day, some facilities will be made available in the Hydraulics Laboratory. These may not be exactly the same as those which will exist on Open Day, and you should be on the alert for any significant differences.

Your device is to extract water from the lower tank and deliver it into the supply pipe inlet. The water will fall from the supply pipe inlet. The performance of your device will be determined by weighing the amount of water delivered in one minute or by timing the delivery of 450 litres if this takes less than one minute.

Instructions and constraints:

1 *Groups:* you will work as far as possible in groups of four (4).

2 *Materials:* your device must be constructed from materials and 'off the shelf' items found in the average suburban hardware store. The use of any type or form of construction kit, ready made pumping device or hoist is expressly not allowed.

3 *Construction Methods:* the device must be constructed using HAND tools only – the use of machine tools is not allowed. Any method of jointing may be used apart from welding, brazing and soldering.

4 *Costing:* all materials used should be costed according to standard size purchased, Where off-cuts etc, are used cost should be the price of the next largest standard commercially available size.

5 *Testing:* each group will have up to three (3) minutes to set up their device. Within this period timing will start when the group is satisfied that their device is working satisfactorily. If the test has not started by the end of the three minute period there will be a penalty deduction of one mark for each ten (10) second delay in getting the test started. The performance of each group will be judged on the average of two test runs, the device being operated by different members of the group in each test. During the test all the operators *must keep their feet on the floor.*

6 *Report:* one report from each group should be submitted one week after final testing. The report should be *concise,* neatly presented in a folder, and should include:

i   An introduction to the design problem
ii   A list of the design concepts considered. (Illustrate with neat sketches.)
iii A description and justification of the concept chosen.
iv   Any design analysis carried out.
v   A statement of the number of man-hours spent on the project.
vi   A complete cost analysis of the device con-structed.
vii A discussion of the performance of your device and your conclusions relating to the overall pro-ject.

7 *Assessment:* as frequently happens with engineering design problems, the final product is required to fulfil a number of criteria, some of which may actually conflict. The most successful design is then the one which is judged to be the best compromise or 'value'. Part of the engineer's task is thus to *optimise* the design specification. In most cases, value judgements are highly subjective and therefore quite variable, but in this project the relative value or 'weighting' of the different design criteria is given by the following system of assessment.

Criterion	Value (marks)	
Creativity of design	10	
Quality of construction	10	
Performance: minimum requirement is that the device must continue to deliver water throughout the two test runs	15	
Competitive performance based on volume of water delivered	35	(max)
Cost (may be negative mark)	15	($)
Report	25	
Total	100	(approx)

The writing of learning experiences as a teaching tool

Professor G.H.A. van Eyk
School of Industrial Design Engineering, Delft
University of Technology

Traditionally, designing can only be taught effectively in small groups by a teacher highly skilled in both design and teaching. Once these conditions are no longer fulfilled, both the motivation of students and of staff, particularly in the 'small' group conditions, dissolve easily. Essential design skills no longer seem to be transferred.

De Groot conceived an interesting new theory broadening explicit educational objectives and encompassing relevant design course objectives – easily forgotten or not easily measurable. It suggests the 'learner report' ('I have learnt that ...' or 'I have learnt how to ...') for solving the 'coverage' problem: 'Is every important objective included?'

This idea is applied to a design course of approximately 150 first year engineering students. At regular intervals students report subjectively on important learning experiences and on individual actions in relation to these experiences. This allows staff to interact more effectively and satisfactorily.

Introduction

In this paper, I describe some experiences with a design course for first year students of the School of Industrial Design Engineering of the Delft University of Technology. To improve the quality of the teaching the students had to write, regularly, short learner's reports. The underlying theories, partly coming from sources published extensively elsewhere (De Groot, 1974, 1975 and 1980) and partly stemming from my own observation, will be discussed and illustrated with examples from the design course. Before going into the theory, I will explain the learner's report: what it is and in what context it should be judged.

What is it, a written learning experience?

The design course of the first year is given by nine staff members to more than 140 students working in groups of five. The course takes one full day per week, for both staff and students, during two semesters of twelve weeks each. The autumn semester comprises three short design exercises and the spring semester is covered by one large exercise. The exercises include all the phases of the design process: information gathering, analysis, synthesis and the making of a prototype that, technically and visually, can be tested: eg a barbecue, a step-ladder or a student's drawing board.

Eight times during the course, at regular intervals, the student is requested to write learning experiences according to the following instructions: one page maximum, typewritten, in the house style. One paragraph on the given task to be able to refresh your memory when re-reading. One paragraph with some learning experiences in the broadest sense. Start your sentence thus: I have learnt that ... (or) how to ... (or)

that it is not always true that ... After doing this three times, a third paragraph has to be added: some specific action related to one or more of your learning experiences: eg next time I will (not) ... .

At the end of both semesters more general learning experiences have to be written after re-reading the earlier ones. All reports together have to be handed in as a booklet in the house style. The reports are only judged on quite formal aspects such as the clarity of the sentences or the specificity of the actions. A common 'error' is that evaluative remarks such as 'I (dis)liked ...' or 'It was highly interesting or boring', are confused with learning effects. Another 'error' is the amalgamation of learning experiences and action. The learning effects and the actions, not being judged, form the basis for the intended dialogue between staff and student.

What was the problem?

The conditions for a traditional design course, small groups and a teacher highly skilled in both design and teaching, were no longer fulfilled when our school saw the number of incoming students exploding from 50 to 144 in five years. There was a growing dissatisfaction with the interaction between student and teacher and we were puzzled as to whether students really learned what we wanted them to learn. As usual with small groups, we had not specified our objectives to the finest detail. Although we were vaguely conscious that every student learns something different during the same exercise, we had no explicit plan or action derived from that consciousness.

Not only dissatisfaction and uncertainty, but also more formal problems were arising: how can we judge the student more objectively? Just from the prototype, or from the reports produced? Do we need to look at the student's process, and if so, at what precisely shall we look? Is it just a 'proper' application of design methodology which can be examined traditionally? All these problems were apparently solved smoothly and unwittingly in the past when the groups were smaller. Large groups, however, like our 144 students, are resistant to these smooth and unwitting solutions.

The large numbers, in my opinion, caused and worsened the problem through four specific factors: (a) Requirements of objectivity prohibit simple parallelisation of a number of small groups. (b) Not all our nine staff members are 'generalists', some are specialists albeit with good understanding of the design profession.[1] (c) The student, being an adolescent in a relatively uncertain situation and having many 'tricks' to get staff to 'tell' him how to proceed, adds to the degrading of the course. I will return to the degrading effect later. (d) The 'irredeemable' attitude of the student to see his teacher more as a judge – to conform to – than as a helper in a process of discovering new insights.[2] The effects (c) and (d) are well known, but in large groups they are more difficult to counteract.

We believed that more precise and detailed learning objectives would surely help us to master the problem. What are we after precisely? Could we find objective test criteria without reducing design to something that can easily be described, tested and operationalised, but which would not be appreciated as proper design by the skilled designer, teacher or, eventually, by industry? The problem, then, could be formulated as follows: 'Can we broaden the learning objectives concept so as to include what we really want to teach and consider relevant,[3] or can we only resort to the traditional small group setting for a satisfying design course?'

De Groot's theory

I found a new theory (De Groot 1974, 1975 and 1980), not particularly made for the design-teaching problem, but broadening the concept of learning objectives and including the learner's report as a crucial element. Learning, De Groot says, results in programmes stored in the memory. These are 'programmes the student can use and steer himself, freely and consciously'.[4] This excludes mental programmes, like conditioning, that cannot be steered and used freely and judiciously. 'The best teachers have always emphasised the importance of insight along with habit formation, as well as the importance of using one's own judgement and that of being free to react otherwise'.[5]

Further, De Groot introduces a classification of all learning objectives based on a double dichotomy: Learners may (report to) have learned either *general* operating *rules* or *particular cases*: exceptions to preconceptions. They may have, further, learned something about the *world*, or, about *themselves*. The resulting four types of learning effects cannot always be measured by ordinary tests, but can be evaluated by various means including 'the use of explicit learner reports'.[6] Figure 1 illustrates the main characteristics of the four cells resulting from the two dichotomies.[7]

The first dichotomy distinguishes the learning of rules from the learning of exceptions: '...learning can be said to proceed from (learning) rules to (learning) exceptions to those rules; then to (learning) new rules encompassing those exceptions; then to (learning) new exceptions to those new rules ...'.[8] The second dichotomy 'grants a status to learning about oneself equal to that of learning about the world'.[9] Learning objectives about oneself are 'conspicuously scarce', says De Groot, but our school, at least, is one of these exceptions. One of its major educational objectives mentions 'self-knowledge' as one of the elements that will enable the student to take full responsibility for his own learning process.[10] The eventual inclusion of 'self-knowledge' in the objectives of the design course

would be nicely backed by that educational objective.

De Groot raises the question whether learning about oneself really belongs to the task of the school or whether the school is doing its duty if it concentrates on objectives of the 'world' only. This is not just a question of ideology: 'higher-order cognitive objectives logically lead[s] to the inclusion of learning about oneself among the goals of School education'.[11]

The application to design education

We are now ready to have a look at the contents of the four cells, A through D, resulting from the dichotomies, and to apply them to design education.

Cell A: The general things of the world. The choice of examples is abundant. Encyclopedias and textbooks offer examples on any page. This is the field where schools traditionally are strongest. Learning objectives of this type can easily be measured and tested. Bureaucratic structures in the university and political pressure from outside tend to restrict the teaching programmes and the objectives to what can be tested and measured 'objectively', which means, restriction to cell A while neglecting the other fields. There is also another mechanism which reduces insight items to cell A objectives: the degrading effect mentioned earlier. Students can be taught to solve problems and answer questions by acquired routine only, without previous insight. 'Teachers, who with the best possible intentions specifically train their students in answering types of test questions, may foster this process of insight items degrading to routine items'.[12] These restrictive effects, that I call 'The Academic Teaching Fallacy',[13] are hard to counteract and deserve, therefore, more attention than they usually receive. To cell A also belong certain specific skills like 'how to operate a typewriter' which can be demonstrated on request and measured to certain standards. In relation to design, cell A is important for useful facts from various fields and rules for finding them. Here, we also find important elementary skills such as how to draw, how to take a photograph or how to make network plans.

Cell B objectives might be expressed as follows: 'there is more to the world – between heaven and earth – than rules for coping with it. ... the riches, the surprises, the unexplained wonders, the exceptions to preconceptions ...'.[11] From an evaluation point of view, cell B objectives pose a problem: exceptions to rules that have been told or taught no longer have surprise value. Teaching of exceptions, on another level, is teaching of rules.

There is also a problem of course development for cell B objectives. Such a course cannot rely on general rules only. Case studies and design exercises seem to include the required surprises. Cell B objectives, in spite of their inherent problems, form a large part of the design course objectives that comply with our ideas about what designing should be: a skilful manipulation of rules and discovering of exceptions to rules by a designer engaged in a learning process in relation to a design problem. A designer has to develop some sense for exceptions; Murphy's Law is a name given to that particular sense.

First year students reported: 'I learned that I cannot make a design by just applying the official norms and standards ... that strength calculus, as learned in the course, is not enough to master the strength problems posed by this 'simple' design ... [and] that there is a separate world, that of the designer's approach to problems'.

Cell C, by definition, should comprise all those objectives which amount to 'learning rules regarding oneself, including one's personal relationships to the world. Again, like in cell A, the "rule" is to include solid facts as well as operating rules for the use of, and adjustment to, objects, instruments, relationships'.[14] In relation to design education, it means that the student has to know his own 'design behaviour', or to be more specific, his 'fact finding behaviour', his 'problem solving behaviour', and so on, to add as an indispensable ingredient to the programmes stored in the memory to be used freely, consciously and judiciously. This type of self-knowledge is invaluable to any designer. It goes beyond knowing one's needs and one's possibilities. It includes also the acquisition of personal programmes – to be steered by oneself – to interact with the world.[15]

Students reported from this type of learning effect: 'I learned that I am quite good at fieldwork/weak at fieldwork', 'I have a tendency to blame myself/others first when things go wrong in the group', 'I tend to linger too much in the fact finding and analysis phase of the design process', 'I start too early/too late with the sketching phase' and 'I work better alone/in groups at the orientation phase'. These learning experiences cannot be 'taught'; most probably they have to be told. Yet they are essential for further devel- opment of a student's design skills. Staff, in general, are experienced enough to understand most of these learning effects and to respond to them adequately.

These learning effects cannot be measured or tested like those of cell A. More like those of cell B these are reportable. De Groot, however, classifies them together with those of cell D as 'communicable', probably in an effort to add an element of 'dialogue' to the word 'reportable'. It is true that some feedback – albeit minimal – is necessary to confirm the learning effect to the student and to bring effective behaviour more consciously into being. The teacher may derive from these 'dialogues' the confirmation that his teachings are effective in accordance with his own objectives and those of the institute he is working for. But, for certain, the dialogue cannot start until the student makes a statement on an individual learning effect.

Cell D, finally, can be expressed as 'taking exception to preconceptions about oneself'.[16] 'Like learning about the world ..., learning about oneself proceeds from rules to exceptions to new rules to new exceptions ....'[17] Although we are far from having a clear picture of how to teach cell D objectives, self- learning about the world cannot proceed, ultimately, without self-learning about oneself, so these objectives are indispensable for a design course.

The learning effects from this cell are a deep source of individual growth and surprise. When listening to great and dedicated designers one will hear quite a few stories, remembered years and years after the event, of surprises about oneself, having caused definite steps in a problem-solving situation. More down-to-earth, our students wrote: 'I have learned that it is *not* true that I have always to rely on other students for finalising my design, ... [that] I can only work successfully when I have got a clear task [and that] ... I can only work with concentration when I have an abundance of time'. These are all exceptions to – restrictive – personal rules, most probably leading to new 'rules' with options to be chosen more freely.

The specific actions

As a teacher – when reading various learning experiences – I felt like asking: 'And what are you going to do with this knowledge?'. When I really did, I discovered to my consternation that quite a few students were *not* intending consciously to use the knowledge during the course: an apparant disjunction of learning and actions. Earlier I had discovered others, who, on the contrary, were hardly able to separate the learning effect from conscious action. In that way they were not free consciously to consider alternatives for further action. These two extremes showed me that the use of the learning effect, if any, would be neither conscious, free, nor judicious. For that reason I required that some specific action should be formulated explicitly in relation to one or more learning experiences. Also here, staff do *not* judge the contents of the action, only its specificity and its relation to a reported learning effect. From the same vein, it is not required that students complete every learning effect with specific action: they will, most probably, develop a sense for using it when appropriate. One student put it as follows in a higher-order learning experience: 'Since I have been noting my learning experiences and actions more consciously, I am much more critical on how to spend my time and attention effectively during a design exer-cise'.

As staff, we cannot 'tell' the student what action is appropriate to a certain learning effect; nor should we try. However, as with learning experiences, feedback from the teacher and some form of dialogue is beneficial, if not essential. Also here, this dialogue cannot start until the student makes a statement about his planned action.

What is the effect?

It is difficult to start, both for staff and students, but it works. Most students write, after some time, learning experiences of all four cells. Design teachers recognise the effect immediately but have difficulty in expressing the learning experiences explicitly: they never had to do it themselves. Students have the same difficulty of formulation but they lack, moreover, the background and understanding that seasoned staff acquire in life. The enormous expansion of the last years, however, has brought us many new staff concerned with many more new problems than just learning experiences. Yet under these difficult circumstances the results are positive. Once staff or students pick up its import, there is enthusiasm. A cell B effect: 'Yes, it is possible and it opens up new ways'. Further development of a theory, suitable for design, is necessary. De Groot's theory seems to be an excellent starting point.

The most hopeful thing, however, is that De Groot's theory, the writing of learning experiences and the writing of action points, is immediately recognised as valuable by design teachers. It is, therefore, a good remedy against various degrading effects that often demotivate design teachers. That will not only help to overcome the remaining difficulties, it will, most of all, improve the quality of the design course. The latter was, after all, the original motivation of the project.

Acknowledgements

The author is grateful to his colleagues of the first year design staff, 1981/1982, and its co-ordinator: Dik Bilderbeek, Cor van Hulten, Fedde van der Meijden, Leo Wartenburgh, Wim Groenenboom, Dico Smit, Kees Kornman and Joost Prins, who, in spite of many uncertainties and lack of clarity at the start, have supported these experiments whole-heartedly.

Figure 1. Classification of all learning objectives according to De Groot.

References

1 As design teachers, we consider the use of specialists to be realistic for the students. In the first year, however, we require staff with an above average understanding of the design profession.

2 At the bottom of this attitude lies the paradox that the university should 'teach freely', while at the same time the result of the examination programme is crucial for the student's place in society later. Grammar School and earlier education contribute heavily to this attitude of looking for answers satisfying the teacher rather than the student himself or the problem.

3 This is the 'coverage' problem, De Groot's main motivation to undertake the relevant studies. De Groot, A. D., 'Categories of educational objectives and effect measures: A new approach discussed in the context of second-language learning', in A. J. van Essen and J. F. Hunting (eds), *The context of foreign-language learning*, Assen, Van Gorcum, 1975, p 39.

4 *Ibid*, p 45.

5 De Groot, A. D., 'To what purpose, to what effect? Some problems of method and theory in the evaluation of higher education'. In: W. A. Verreck (ed.), *Methodological problems in research and development in higher education,* Proceedings of the inaugural EARDHE-Congress, Rotterdam, December 1973. Amsterdam, Swets and Zeitlinger, 1974, p 30.

6 *Ibid*, p 17.

7 This diagram is derived from De Groot 1974, *op cit*, p 34; 1975, *op cit,* p 47; and: De Groot, 'Over leerervaringen en leerdoelen', in *Handboek Onderwijspraktijk,* Afl 10, November 1980, Band I, deel II p 16. The latter is slightly different from earlier diagrams.

8 De Groot 1975, p 49. The interaction between a designer and his design can be described – at least partially – as a learning process of this type.

9 *Ibid* p 50.

10 The second objective of the second order says: 'At the end of the 5 year course the engineer ID has obtained insight in the theoretical and philosophical basic principles of the fields mentioned above, and the self-knowledge, so as to be able, at least, to evaluate, to accept or to reject newly offered knowledge thus to be capable of taking full responsibility for his own learning processes as a professional engineer.'

11 De Groot 1975, *Op cit,* p 51.

12 *Ibid*, p 41. He refers to Otto Selz (1922) for a particular formulation of this effect in terms of general and specific problem solving methods.

13 I phrased it 'The Academic Teaching Fallacy' to express the false notion that our universities offer, as a matter of course, the most complete education possible.

14 De Groot 1975, p 52.

15 De Groot 1980 *op cit*, p 9.

16 *Ibid*, p 15.

17 De Groot 1975, *op cit,* p 54.

18 I suspect that a dominant learning/teaching culture, mainly aiming at performing well at examinations, has generated the 'rule' that 'learning is for examinations, not for life'.

19 Typical example: 'I learned that I will never use squared paper for my sketches again'. Apparently there has been a negative experience but this type of reaction seems to belong to 'conditioning' rather than to reflective learning of programmes applied consciously, freely and judiciously.

20 See also: Selz, O. *Zur Psychologie des produktiven Denkens und des Irrtums, eine experimentelle Untersuchung.* Fr. Cohen, Bonn, 1922.

Experimental design: an antidote to the design process

Avram Grant
Centre for Technological Education, Holon, Israel

Hypothesis

Current trends are reducing the design process to a series of procedural exercises aided by advanced technology.

This trend dehumanises the process and deprives designers of their greatest assets: inspiration and creativity.

To ensure that design remains a creative activity, we must develop an antidote to the current trend in the design process.

Argument

One must beware of overdependency on scientific design methods. Most design which converges on 'optimal' middle of the road solutions is often defined 'acceptable', 'satisfactory' or 'justified' but rarely regarded as 'bold', 'imaginative' or 'outstanding'. Past efforts systematically to increase creativity were directed towards practising or non-design professionals (example: Brainstorming, Synectics, etc). However the opportunity to encourage creativity and instil its accompanying sensations of excitement and reward is during design education.

Resolve

A modest contribution to this goal is our course Experimental Design. It is structured in deliberate contrast with most acceptable concepts of design processes.

Assignments range from ridiculous to seemingly impossible and solutions are founded on intuition, trial and error or intellectual whim.

The course is unscientific, unmethodical, unsystematic, yet very exciting, remarkably productive and extremely rewarding.

It is an antidote to the design process.

Introduction

One can notice a trend developing within the design community. Those involved – the designers, researchers and educators in design – know it well. It is not a matter of an international style emerging. The similarity of style is merely the symptom, the matter on hand is much more fundamental and concerns our future role in the activity we presently term 'design'. The establishment and entrenchment of the systems approach in design and the introduction of computer aided design is casting serious doubts on the role of the individual designer and the need for his creative genius.

The following statements of observation have been formulated to serve as guidelines for a course in design education. They also serve as the hypothesis for this paper.

Hypothesis

The design process is gradually being reduced to a series of procedural activities aided by advanced computerised technology, all, of course, in the name of progress.

The increasing trend towards fully computerised and strictly methodical approaches in design reduces the designers' involvement and sense of responsibility, thus leading to the de-humanisation of the design process.

This trend inevitably deprives many designers of the realisation of their greatest assets which are their inspiration and creativity.

To assure that design remains in the domain of creative human activity it is essential to develop an antidote to the current trend in design processes.

Argument

'The only constant phenomenon of life is change ... .'

An anonymous quotation so true to the world of design. Only the ignorant, the superstitious and the religious fanatic attempt to obstruct change, usually with little success. This presentation is certainly not a crusade against the inclusion of design methodology or the aids of advanced technology in the design process. One should not obstruct progress in modern society, especially not in an area so open and conducive to change as design.

However, 'progress' has repeatedly resulted in grave adverse effects, for example: the convenience of our car is the greatest contributor to air pollution, preservatives and flavouring additives which seemingly enhance our food are hazardous to our health, fertilisers and insecticides which are used to increase agricultural crops are a threat to the ecology. Hence one must be wary of indiscriminately accepting 'progress' for its own sake.

Several observations are especially alarming: as designers become more and more dependent on the techniques and mechanics of their trade, the human aspects of design will assume a secondary role. The designer may soon become technology's slave rather than its master.

We suspect that scientific design methods and computer aided design lead to the increasing similarity in design. If so and if unchecked, we will soon find ourselves surrounded by a visually monotonous world, regardless of how elegant or efficient each single statement might be.

The sophisticated hardware and the knowledge for its application in design are in the possession of only the few who can afford it. Can we honestly claim to be attempting to close the gap between the advanced and the developing societies?

Having recognised the impending development, we must prepare for it. What can be done to remedy the dangers of this trend? What can we in design education offer to our students to bolster their commitment to design as a human activity on a human scale with all related challenges and rewards?

Resolve

Design education must therefore increase its efforts to stimulate intellectually its students, to excite, to challenge and to reward them with the kind of experiences that are becoming rare in the professional environment. In our effort to develop an educational tool that will promise a lasting effect, we looked around for similar attempts in other fields. Science and medicine have long ago mastered the development of antidotes for various ailments. The term 'antidote' itself was excellent for our purpose. However its duplication and application in design is not very practical. In a completely different vein, we noted how the French and the Italians prepare for the task of consuming a sumptuous meal – they have invented the antipasto and the aperitif. These delightful forms of nourishment precede the meal, yet have very little in common with either its contents or its character.

Eureka! If design practice with its methods and processes is our main meal, we must serve an antipasto before it!

Translated into practical terms in our own field, this presents a challenge to develop a course which is very different from accepted norms of design education and design practice. And since design today is increasingly scientific, methodical and systematic, our course must be deliberately unscientific, non-methodical and unsystematic. We have therefore devised assignments that range from the ridiculous to the seemingly impossible and their solutions could not be planned, plotted or figured out in advance. Consequently, in coping with the assigned problems, students had to rely on intuition, trial and error, intellectual whim and experimentation.

The title of our course is 'Experimental Design'. Like a good antipasto it must tease our appetite, awaken our taste buds and reward us with its rich variety before we bring on the pasta!

Experimental Design

Example: m²
'Design with one square meter' was the given assignment. The criteria called for ingenuity and originality in the application of a two-dimensional material, stretching it to exceed its traditional applications and if possible to challenge credibility.

The results included some true fruits of fantasy like a lady's matching hat and handbag made of cake

frosting, dinnerware of candied sugar and a basket for and of lasagna noodles. Paper received prominent treatment and provided an assortment of products including house slippers, a disposable waste basket, spill-proof drinking cups and a facsimile attaché case. Other materials provided a PVC sculpture defining a ball in space, a giant veneer clothespin, and a wire mesh vest and sculptures. The 'coolest' entry was a window with panes made of sheets of ice; it lasted half an hour.

Figure 1.
Project: a basket for and of lasagna noodles.

Example: Senseless

'Explore our senses and design a device to confuse one of them'. No other guidelines or criteria were given! Obviously, vision, on which we rely the most, was the easiest to confuse in many ways. Devices were developed to invert, distort, avert direction and reflect images in various angles. Hearing, too, received its share of attention. One attempt was to make it more selective by enabling it to detect direction, another proposal was to use it in speech training to control the volume of the voice. Even touch, taste and smell received a most original and amusing treatment.

Example: Body design

'Design a product which is obviously intended for the human body.' This project required some enquiry and research by each student to determine what part of the body to treat. Hardly any area of our body was neglected. Products were developed for the hands and legs, for the hips, back, shoulder and armpits, as well as for neck and various elements in our head – nose, ears, etc.

The foot was exercised, tickled and cooled by various devices. The hand was braced and supported to perform its strenuous tasks better. Designs for the back and shoulders were intended to increase their efficiency and diversity in work. Other products were aimed at correcting posture in various positions. For the elbow there was a crowd defender and for the underarms an elegant bellows for cooling and ventilation. Special decorations and ornaments were designed for the ears, the nose, and even for that embarrassing bald spot on our head. The seat received special attention with the development of new seating devices which totally alleviated the pressure on our delicate tissues. Indeed, we witnessed an explosion of information in concept, shape and function.

Figure 2.
Project: designing products obviously intended for the human body.

Conclusion
The seemingly entertaining atmosphere of this course was balanced by a good measure of hard work, trial and error, of frustration and struggle for new design. The intention was to maintain the assignments on a conceptual level, to brainstorm the problems not only verbally but also visually and three-dimensionally. However, the solutions often proposed remarkably practical ideas.

The entire experiment and exchange were developed as a design activity which averts the tedious and boring aspects of product development, in order to concentrate on the excitement of invention and the rewards of idea materialisation. In addition, interdisciplinary activities which were conducted in conjunction with this course contributed to the positive attitude and the continuous flow of original ideas.

'Experimental Design' proved to be a most rewarding experience to all participants.

Bibliography

Barnard, Christian, *The Body Machine,* Hamlyn, 1981.
Dreyfuss, Henry, *Designing for People,* Viking, New York, 1974.
Ghiselin, Brewster, *The Creative Process,* Mentor, New York.
Gordon, William J.J. *Synectics*, Collier MacMillan, New York, 1968.
Jones, J. Christopher, *Design Methods,* John Wiley & Sons, London, 1970.
Gregory, R.L. *Eye and Brain,* London, 1966.
Gregory, R.L. *The Intelligent Eye,* London, 1970.

Design education for industrial managers

Roger A. Gale
Smallpeice Trust Limited, Southampton

We are today educating designers whose working lives could extend into the 2020s. What will they need as a basis for their careers? What technologies must we teach so that they have potential in that future world? How best can we fit them for a world which we cannot know?

These are the normal questions which are asked. Is this then what industry wants or needs, or should we train people to use their creative and intellectual abilities more fully? We have a creative and intellectual potential from the day we are born until the day we die, which we do not make full use of. How can design managers and educationalists help develop more fully this potential for the betterment of the common good?

In the world today the ambition of every nation seems to be to have a technological base to enable that country to become industrialised. To do this the country will entice a multi-national firm or firms into its country normally because of the cheap labour which is available. By having these firms in the country it is hoped then that people will be encouraged to become engineers. Technical schools, colleges and universities will be opened. This again will be imported by sending people to a Western or Soviet University. The information which is brought back becomes the basis for the education of a country's future engineers. The schooling then is a replica of a foreign system and not indigenous. The system initially employed might not be the best for the country. Once installed, however, it becomes difficult to change. The more so as the engineers produced under this system become the lecturers of tomorrow.

At this point, I think it is time to take a long look at what we are trying to achieve and are achieving in our training of engineers, what we perhaps should be trying to achieve, how and when engineering should be taught and what an engineer is anyway.

To take the last question first. What is an engineer?

The United Kingdom has been an industrial nation longer than most. This was because we needed machines to enable us to make the products which we would export all around the world. The coming of the steam engine both stationary and locomotive did not only change the face of the British Isles it also gave another meaning to the word 'engineer'. The Stevensons were engineers. Brunel was an engineer as was Charles Parsons.

Initially the term engineer meant the person who *engineered* the machines, ie the person who designed the machine which would fulfil a particular task. In those early days, the person who operated the machine had to overcome the problems as he went along. It is not surprising therefore that the term engineer now applies to any person using a machine in the engineering industry. Due to this we now have a problem when it comes to the training of engineers. If we talk to the general public about an engineer, what do they see? They will see a person making or assembling motor cars. They will see the person who has just repaired their television set or the person maintaining their motor car. What they will not see is the person at the drawing board trying to get the optimum solution to a problem. Yet this is what an engineer really is. The word engineer has its roots in the word *ingineer* which meant a person of ingenuity. This person was originally employed by kings and nobles to design engines of war.

Thus an engineer is a person who can solve engineering problems. We have therefore electronic engineers, mechanical engineers, pneumatic engineers and so on. In many organisations the word design has been added to the term engineer to indicate a difference between 'engineers'. We thus confuse the situation still further by having electronic design engineers, mechanical design engineers, pneumatic design engineers etc. Irrespective of the name their one common aspect is that they are all problem solvers. They must, by the very nature of their work, be able to be either given a problem or perceive a problem and then arrive at a solution which is economically viable and fulfils all that is asked of it.

Having ascertained that an engineer is a thinker and a solver of problems, I feel it is time to see how he becomes an engineer.

In most cases an interest will show in things mechanical or electrical so an apprenticeship might be obtained during which a certain amount of Engineering Drawing is taught. The apprentices with the most aptitude in the technical skills will be selected for further advancement and so into the drawing and design office. During the training they will be taught about the strength of materials, how to calculate the stress and strain in a material, about tolerances and the principles of costing and much more. At the end of the course an examination will be set. Having passed the examination and armed with a certificate there is another course which will lead to more qualifications and ultimately to more financial rewards.

Another rigorous path can be taken by a person who is highly academically qualified. He or she can avail themselves of the opportunity to attend a university. Having chosen a university, the individual will be given a wealth of new knowledge and information to enable that person to obtain a degree. Armed with this document he or she will, depending on grade, either move into industry or stay at university to obtain an MSc. Depending on the ability of the student he or she will then continue at university perhaps as a research fellow or lecturer, or go into industry.

This is a summary of the design engineering education system which is common to countries around the world. Whether we like it or not the individual's and the training establishment's creditability rely on the number of passes achieved and the grades of those passes. This is not only noticeable in the technical schools and universities, it is also the same in our secondary education. It appears then that we are training students to pass examinations so that at the end of the 'year' we can pat them on the back and say 'well done, you have passed'.

Dr E. Paul Torrance in an article said that 'if we were to identify children as gifted on the basis of intelligence or scholastic aptitude tests, we would eliminate from consideration approximately 70 per cent of the most creative'.[1]

This is obviously not the declared aim of any educational organisation. In the long term however, this must be the outcome. We are giving students, over the years, vast amounts of knowledge. The practice is that we find out whether the information has been memorised by giving a test. In reality then, although we set out to create engineers, we create people who are very good at retrieving information. They have good memories. Having a good memory does not in itself mean there is the inherent ability to apply the information thus stored.

George Stephenson (1781–1848) once said of examinations 'you should never judge a goose by its stuffing'.

George Stephenson was an engineering genius with a distinct advantage. He could apply the information; in other words, he could *think*.

In acknowledging the fact that we need information and that must be obtained by being taught, I feel that we should not make the assumption that the students are capable of using the information thus given. In today's world many politicians and governments are coming to the conclusion that the only way to create jobs is to create new products and new industries. There is a need to innovate, to invent or in other words to design.

I say to design because designing is the application of knowledge and experience to solve a problem and to turn that solution into a product. The product then is the tangible representation of a person's thoughts. The product can range from dresses to paper towels, from missiles to saucers, which sometimes fly. The common denominator is that they were designed. Some individual or group through thinking, through applying their knowledge, arrived at a solution to a problem. It does not matter whether we are called electronic designers, mechanical designers or have any other title that can be given. The very fact that thought is needed to produce a result is the unifying element throughout the engineering spectrum. This seems to be a reasonable supposition. After all, we cannot assume there is a mental or physical difference between an electronic and a mechanical engineer just because of their different disciplines.

Unless special training is given to aid the solving of problems, the majority of design engineers think along the same lines. There are many reasons for this but the main one seems to be the education system. Mostly the education is very methodical and the children are encouraged to conform. This can be most easily illustrated in the Japanese education system. In Japan at a given time on a given day, all the children taking a subject, say physics, will be working on exactly the same thing. The Japanese system then is very rigid and formal. This has led to the Japanese being very poor inventors.

This fact has been highlighted in three ways. Firstly, in 1981 a Japanese White Paper[2] compared Japan's 'epochal breakthroughs' with the technological innovations of Britain, the United States, and West Germany. The Japanese say that they have achieved 7.7 per cent of such breakthroughs. Secondly the head of Sony research, Dr Makoto Kikuchi, stated on the BBC television programme Horizon that 'we can do something once we get the clear target ... we can concentrate our work on one thing together'. Lastly in December 1981 Kenichi Fukui received the joint Nobel prize for original research in chemistry. He was the fourth Nobel prize winner in Japanese history.

It is imperative that we maintain our abilities to be creative. The problem is that we are tending away from this. When I say 'we' I mean the world as a whole. To understand the reasons for this trend, I will briefly mention one aspect of creative design which deals with the brain.

It is now generally accepted that the brain is divided into compartments which specialise in various functions. There is an interaction between the areas of the brain and some functions of one part can be transferred to another. For example, the left hand side of the brain can take over some of the functions of the right and vice versa. The functions of mathematics, analysing, logic and language are the responsibilities of the left side. This side is normally dominant because it is the side most used for writing and manipulation, in other words, we are right handed. The left controls the right side of the body and the right side the left side of the body. The right side of the brain is the creative side. In this side the functions of creativity, musical appreciation, spatial awareness and general emotions are assimilated. The problem is that as a society becomes more technologically oriented, then that society uses the left hand side of the brain more and more. As the left is dominant in the first place, that dominance is reinforced throughout our years of training and then in the offices and organisations for which we work. It is not surprising then, that we become very good at logical thinking and poor at innovating and spatial awareness. It was not always that way. At one time the majority of people had the ability to be original but due to various pressures both physical and psychological we have lost that ability. If we are to maintain the rate of progress which we have enjoyed over the years, then it is vital that we revive that ability. I say revive. It is only possible to revive something which is not dead. The longer it has lain dormant then the longer the revival will take.

We should, during our training of engineers, not just concentrate on the practical side of engineering, we must teach engineers how to apply the information and thus improve their creativity. If we do this we gain an engineer who not only has the knowledge, but can apply that knowledge. He can think. This ability to think not only produces better ideas but due to the way the brain stores information makes engineers more able to retain the facts which are presented to them. We also gain a person who can assimilate new facts and does not become stereo-typed. He maintains the ability to adapt to changing situations and therefore does not resist change because it might affect his position.

One problem with the teaching of thinking to engineers is that it is very difficult to examine. The examination of creativity is possible but difficult. The decision of whether to examine is quite fundamental to the exercise. I feel that it is mainly practice that is needed. After the theory has been explained then the more practice the more able that person is when applying that theory.

The late Sir Barnes Wallis said of his schooling 'I knew nothing except how to think, how to grapple with a problem and then to go on grappling with it until you had solved it'.[3] This ability to think creatively was demonstrated at the Bielefeld Viaduct during the Second World War. The Americans dropped 3000 tons of bombs trying to hit and destroy the target. Barnes Wallis said that instead of trying to hit the viaduct, they should miss it with a bomb which would create an earthquake. Thus a ten ton 'earthquake' bomb was designed and the viaduct destroyed.

Having discussed the problem of thinking now comes the problem of teaching it.

This is nearly a 'Catch 22' situation. The people who must teach it are naturally the teachers. The teachers were taught that to conform is right and that there is only one answer to a problem, 'the right one'. The circle will continue to turn unless or until something is done to break that circle. It is possible to make a start in respect to this country through the CNAA (Council for National Academic Awards) to make it compulsory in Teacher Training Colleges. This would have the advantage that children between five and eight years of age would continue to be exposed to a creative environment. As the child progressed through schooling the ability to create would be nurtured so that in the long term we would have creative adults. This is looking at the long term solution to the problem. The results would not be seen for some 15 years.

Before moving on, Dr Eugene Curie said of his son Pierre that he was 'too original to be a brilliant pupil'.[4] This illustrates, I think, a point understood for many years: the fact that a brilliant academic ability does not in itself mean a person is highly creative.

In the short term we must endeavour to teach our present design staff how to think and then encourage them to do just that. This is the design manager's sphere of influence. It is the design manager's decision as to whether to enact any new programme in his organisation. If he does decide to train his designers in the art of problem solving then the designers will become better at their jobs. As with teachers, he should be able to recognise creativity and to give assistance when needed.

The design manager can start by making his staff aware of the various aspects of problem solving and of thinking techniques in general. This can be done by the manager himself or by an outside source. In some respects it is better for the manager to do it because he knows the product and the problems associated with that product. Generally though, it is preferred to take advantage of an outside source. The reason for this is that the outside source is perhaps more able to advise and instruct the staff.

During the course the designers would be introduced to methods of ideas generation and the problems associated with analysing a new idea. The ideas generation stage is when we need to think *divergently*. We must not analyse any idea. During our training however, this is what we are trained to do. We tend to think of one or two ideas and immediately analyse those ideas. If those ideas are non-productive it becomes very difficult to achieve more. The analysing of an idea is called convergent thinking. During this stage we select an idea and by using our experience and knowledge, turn it into a practical proposition. At this stage again a very important and very difficult situation occurs. This is when the logical nature which we possess is important ie the logical development of a product. The problem is that at this stage we need to innovate. This may take the form of new or unusual fixings, new materials, methods of manufacture, new electronic systems control, etc.

It can be seen then that the designer needs to be two people. Firstly at the ideas stage he is an innovator and illogical thinker. Secondly, he becomes a judge. He is a logical thinker who can take an idea and develop that idea. As I have already stated, we are excellent at creating the latter but not the former. In indicating that the designer needs to be two people, it is possible for two people to work as a team. One could be the innovator and the other the implementor. This system can work very well providing the two people are compatible.

The design manager can help in other ways which can have a very marked effect on the designer. The designer must be praised for his achievements. So many managers feel unable to praise for a job well done. If the atmosphere in the office can become one in which it is not a catastrophe to be wrong then more ideas will be produced. One of the greatest inducements to being creative is to develop an atmosphere where designers are not frightened of producing concepts which might seem silly. The joint fears of failure and ridicule is one of the crosses that designers bear.

In conclusion, I have not dealt with the attitude, still around, that many people have towards change: the unjustified fear and sometimes open hostility shown by people towards innovation. Also the actual training techniques, although tried and tested, would take far too long to explain here. I have shown that there is an area of education which, although fundamental to all fields of engineering, is not freely available to engineers. That area is the one of the problem solving and thinking techniques. It is however, an area which many countries admit is in need of improvement. We cannot educate designers today in disciplines which they will need in 20 years' time because we do not know what will be needed in 20 years. What we can and must do, is to teach them how to think so they make better use of their intellectual abilities. This is being done on a small scale but it should be on a national or international level.

A final quote I give to Carl H. Grabo.

'Considering man's hostility to change and innovation ... it is astonishing that so much creative and imaginative genius has contrived to leave its impression on the human race. Yet who can doubt that more habited in weak bodies blasted early by ignorance and superstition, has perished with no record? In our comparatively low civilisation, a little is done under favourable circumstances to salvage great talent, to give it opportunity to grow and express itself. Yet how pitifully meagre is our salvage and how great the waste! We know that this is so.

'A more civilised time than ours will strive to develop this, the greatest of all natural resources.'[5]

Carl Grabo wrote that in 1948. Let us hope that the 'more civilised time' starts at The Design Policy Conference 1982.

References

1   Torrance, Dr E. Paul, 'The Creative Child' *Look*, 1962.
2   Bulletin of the Anglo-Japanese Economic Institute, No 225, July – August 1981.
3   Whitfield, P.R. *Creativity In Industry*, Penguin Books, 1975.
4   Curie, Eve, *Madame Curie*, Heinemann, 1938 (reprinted 1962).
5   Grabo, C. H. *The Creative Critic*, University of Chicago Press.

Curriculum development in design at further education level

R.C. Sale
Chelsea School of Art, UK

This paper describes what are seen as the dilemmas and issues of current educational practice in industrial design. It examines the theory and values underpinning curriculum design and teaching methods, especially the model of professional practice on which much educational work is dependent, the project method of teaching and techniques of assessment.

There is very little development work in this field and the author identifies what he sees as inhibitory factors to growth and change in practice. The paper is a practitioner's account and in this sense is seen as a contribution to a debate on the possibilities of change which is long overdue.

Stenhouse has described curriculum development as 'an attack on the separation between theory and practice'.[1] In industrial design education this can be seen as the distance between what we assume the characteristics of the educational model are and what they really are.

Taking Roberts'[2] concept of the model 'one' and model 'two' curriculum usefully illuminates this dilemma. Model 'one' is past-orientated, learning seen as an accumulation of necessary skills through practice and an external transmission of values, knowledge and methods, whereas model 'two' is future orientated; it is developmental, centres on processes of learning, sees learning as reciprocal action between individuals and is concerned with the personal construction and reconstruction of knowledge, values and skills. The emphasis of model two is on personal inquiry and action in practice and not on a theoretical structure of symbolic procedures.

It was seen that industrial design education has been claiming much of the ground of 'model two' while practising substantially within 'model one'. That is, identifying with the inquiring and critical qualities of design activity while containing it at arm's length. As Roberts points out the concept of two models creates a useful dialectic for discussion through which the popular base of practice can be questioned and it was from this inquiring approach that a curriculum development project was initiated at Chelsea School of Art during the 1980/81 academic session.

The project addressed what were seen as inherent issues and dilemmas of educational practice. Motivation came from concern that a mismatch appeared to be developing between preparing students to be effective designers, able to think, act, evaluate and sustain a viable working future in an environment whose main characteristic is change; and the rather passive and static model of industrial design practice which is promoted through the methods and conventions of educational practice.

The model of professional practice was questioned as the sole source for the development of the curriculum. The model was seen to impose a view of design practice which was unnecessarily doctrinaire and uncharacteristic of what designers do in the field and how design activity 'feels', limiting the growth of the curriculum and in some instances inhibiting personal learning, knowing and doing.

For example the claims that are made for the project method seem to fit well with design activity; the release the method affords from the authoritarian role of teaching and the opportunity it provides for integration and development of knowledge, skill and experience across subject disciplines in 'natural' forms of learning. This approach is particularly relevant in a discipline like industrial design which is often dealing with ill-defined 'problems'. The method's exploratory character and the focus that this places on the student in sustaining and evaluating his/her own learning are well known.[3]

However it is the observation of the author that the industrial design educational project can become the vehicle through which the model of practice drives the curriculum to the extent that it distorts the very qualities that are seen as the advantages of the method. Formalised structure and conventional teaching intervention can be to the detriment of exploration and disclosure of the subject at hand and to the student's potential in that situation.

Industrial design practice is success orientated. Within this context it is possible to perceive design activity as a rational 'results' producing process. When pressure of time and pressure to 'succeed' reinforce the complete primacy of the end product as the unit of design and education assessment, several dilemmas arise. In the rush to produce an answer some of the understanding of how the design activity 'works' may be lost. This can be problematic if proper time is not allowed for feedback and developmental work when this is seen to be necessary by either teacher or student. 'End-on' projects may even work to reinforce weaknesses in understanding, skill etc if these aspects are not intelligently separated.

For instance, 'effectiveness' in industrial design education is not only concerned with issues which can be measured in quantifiable terms. Industrial designers address themselves to as many issues of a qualitative kind, meaning, perception, value etc, which are less accessible to development through conventional teacher/learning encounters of industrial design education and which may also require different approaches to measure.

Pressure for results may have other effects. The student may choose to make a product which is suitable for tidy assessment rather than maximising learning and may be reluctant to externalise or focus on work processes, strategies and approaches for observation and reflection. The influence of the model of practice can also lead to confusion between educational aims and 'end-product'. In areas of manipulative skill development the issues are easier to separate but confusion can arise where subsidiary aims concerned with conceptual, judgemental and discriminatory tasks or with the development of methods of approach and evaluation are considered the most important in the project. The failure of a student to reach the focal aims of a project does not necessarily indicate that it has been unsuccessful. In this situation attaining understanding through design action or sustaining design activity within an agreed conceptual structure may be far more valuable indicators of the 'success' and usefulness of the project to the student than attainment of the focus.

Pressure for results produces the attitude that the design of the curriculum is only the proper concern of the teacher; it neglects that the curriculum is constructed out of the student's interpretation of its intentions and that the student is well placed to identify his or her own needs, contribute to the evaluation of his or her learning and to the development of the curriculum. It can be argued that the purpose of industrial design education is to lead the student *away* from dependence on external evaluation and to prepare students to construct their own framework for evaluating design action and decisions.

The curriculum project was designed to be exploratory in nature, its main objective being to achieve sufficient 'movement' within the *status quo* of practice to allow new thoughts and ideas to be tested, towards constructing a broader, more informed personal perspective from which to continue development. The concept of 'creative-disturbance' that Jones[4] attributes to design is perhaps an apposite description. The idea of exploratory work in curriculum development raises several issues. If the exploration is to be real it would not make sense to predict what is going to be found. On the other hand to prescribe aims in great detail would undermine its learning potential. The stance that was taken was to acknowledge that at the planning stage, aims, intended outcomes, and issues would be anticipated but that there would be those which would come out of or be modified by fulfilling the plan, which could not be anticipated.

Shifts in practice intended through the project were inter-dependent to some extent and can be fitted into three broad categories:

1 *To develop the project form.*
   The conventional form based on a professional assignment was reassessed and forms derived appropriate to address a wider range of learning tasks within the discipline. The focally aimed project resulting in a tangible outcome was not

rejected but a shift towards a balance with subsidiary aims was attempted.
2 *To give inquiry into the nature of design and designing a proper 'place' within the curriculum.*
   The intention was to make the process of designing 'showable' so that design strategies and methods could be explored and developed.
3 *To shift the teacher/student relationship away from authoritarian dependence.*
   To bring the student away from complete dependence on external evaluation and to external 'standards' towards a position where the student is able to think, act and evaluate from the locus of themselves and within the terms of reference of the exercise. This aspect has considerable and far-reaching implications on the day-to-day activities and planning of the exercises.

The project was structured as a programme of 'exercises' built into a normal pattern of end-on design projects. Although each 'exercise' had different educational aims there were attributes which they all held in common:

1 Each exercise focused on a single aspect of industrial design learning, exploring issues within that area. Attention was diminished on other aspects wherever these were considered not to be significant to the development of understanding and practice.
2 Subjects were chosen for their contentious, or problematic nature. These were aspects which were considered difficult to penetrate within the boundaries set by conventional 'design assignment' project forms but were nevertheless considered central to the discipline. The following is a list of examples of issues addressed through the 'exercises':

   a poor understanding and utilisation of ergonomic data by industrial designers
   b nature of the 'fit' between marketing and industrial design in the consumer product area
   c place of personal values and meaning in industrial design
   d language of detail and form on products (concept of design 'handwriting')
   e colour/form values and relationships.

3 The exercises worked on two levels, being concerned with 'how' to learn while pursuing 'what' to learn. To reinforce this process each student was required to make a trace of the inquiries and strategies adopted en route.
4 The exercises shifted students towards greater responsibility for their own learning: for example, to contribute to the evaluation of their own learning, methods of working, evidence produced and development of the exercise. Allowance was

made for 'in-progress' adjustments to the structure, content and direction of any 'exercise' in response to feed-back.

5   Each 'exercise' was dependent on a raised temperature of inquiry. This was achieved by a high level of interaction between teachers and students throughout. Such methods as sub-group working, cross-group discussion, group seminars and teacher collaboration in the student task were employed.

6   Each exercise sought to achieve a proper relationship between focal and subsidiary aims. The view was taken that although the end product can easily become the most obvious candidate for assessment, it may not be the most important outcome of the project for the learner. Learning aims were established which involved measurement of changes in a student's understanding, abilities, knowledge etc which were not solely assessable through teacher-centred evaluation of the product.

7   The exercises had a short time span, from one to five days.

Shift in the teacher/student relationship was crucial to the development of the project. The structure of the conventional industrial design project reflects the ambivalence of the relationship. Great significance and impact can be placed on key points like briefing and final assessment, ensuring the role of teacher as expert.

Assumptions were made during the project that the student had the ability and need to learn and was able to make a valuable contribution to the construction and assessment of this process, and that the characteristics and quality of design activity in an area like industrial design demand an open and collaborative learning environment.

Emphasis in this relationship is on the teacher working to further each student's understanding of the nature of his or her inquiry and to explore its aims. While advice and contribution is made by the teacher to the inquiry, he nevertheless accepts that the student is the master of his or her own situation. This approach does not deny nor depend on focal objectives, approval from teachers, external separate assessment or pressure of timed programmes for its effectiveness.

Teachers in this kind of relationship have to expect that the student is also well placed to assess the intention of any part of the curriculum, its design, teaching input and resource.

Written and other forms of record can be made by both student or teacher at agreed points or stages of the inquiry. The teacher is able to perceive the quality of understanding and management of skill-learning a

student is exercising 'in action' at any chosen point of the process.

The rewards of confronting issues in a quest to determine what questions are worth asking can be considerable to both teacher and student. It may bring *both* on to ground which is unfamiliar providing the teacher and student equal opportunity to learn and increase their perceptions and understanding within the reality of the inquiry. Although the teacher's wider repertoire of strategies may be useful in suggesting an overall structure to the inquiry, his or her knowledge of precedent solutions may be of no more advantage than what the student is able to construct within the inquiry.

A design project based on this type of teaching relationship cannot be unreal or 'academic'. Projects become vehicles for speculation and research permitting teacher and student to look deeply into a subject by putting together and testing out methods of handling the inquiry as these are seen to be necessary. Stenhouse in his article, 'The Humanities Curriculum Project', called this approach 'inquiry based teaching'.

An *inquiry based approach* has advantages when it is applied to industrial design teaching:

1   It makes the evaluation of subsidiary aims possible in a case where these are of greater importance than the focal outcome in measuring a student's development within a design project. They may include behavioural and conceptual aspects, for instance, how a student decided what to do at a stage of a project, ways of working developed, how he or she managed working with others, transfer of understanding knowledge and skills from previous work, etc.

2   The student is learning to think and act within the discipline in his or her own terms. By placing emphasis on the process of inquiry and construction of evidence of this, the student becomes more conscious of the nature of design activity and is, therefore, more able to evaluate his or her own development and more accurately evaluate any outcomes from that process within terms of the process. This provides a far better basis for personal development as it brings how a student works and his or her own learning difficulties into open dialogue, with the student being able to make a direct contribution to this. It also allows students to identify those techniques, strategy and methods that worked well for them and extract from the situation principles which could be applied into other situations.

3   The teacher by his involvement in the inquiry is able to support and ratify the analysis that the student is able to make at assessment stages, and give advice which is perceptive, relevant and fits into continuity of development.

What was essential in this approach was that from the outset both staff and students agreed on aims, and where emphasis of assessment was to be placed in the project.

It is the view of the author that involving students in discussion about the intention and structure of the curriculum has inherent values for both teachers and students:

1   It makes sure that there is shared understanding about what is expected, the purpose and sense of a project.
2   That the curriculum is seen to be accessible and responsive to change.
3   That the curriculum maintains relevance and continuity.
4   It reflects the need for terms of reference in design activity.
5   It creates a precedent for an open dialogue which can be developed further throughout the curriculum.
6   It places responsibility for the inquiry with the student.

References

1   Stenhouse, L. *An Introduction to Curriculum Research and Development*, Boaks (ed), Heinemann, UK, 1975, p 3.
2   Roberts, P. *Beyond the Stable School* (paper) Royal College of Art, London, 1979.
3   Adderley, Ashley, Baldwin (*et al*), *Project Methods in Higher Education*, Society of Research into Higher Education, UK, 1977, p 14.
4   Jones, J.C. '... in the dimension of time', *Design Studies*, no 3, 1980, pp 172–176.

Local curriculum development in environmental education

Eileen Adams
Design Education Unit, Royal College of Art, UK

Ken Baynes introduced Eileen Adams by giving a brief history of the Art and the Built Environment Project:

When the Royal College of Art was engaged on its Design in General Education study for the Department of Education and Science, the project team found that the great mass of design activity in schools was directed at product or graphic design. Schools were interested in environmental studies but these were seen through the perspectives of history, geography, natural and social science; architecture and planning were almost totally neglected. The team argued that a study of the environment was absolutely fundamental to the development of design awareness and that if no work of this kind was going on, they must invent some. From this conviction came the Frontdoor project, based at Pimlico School and involving co-operation between the ILEA, the architects of the Greater London Council and the Royal College of Art.

Frontdoor ran from 1974 to 1976. It showed that the study of buildings and places could be pursued through the art curriculum and that architects and planners could work with teachers to devise study methods and share their expertise on the aesthetic and design aspects of townscape. It showed that children were strongly motivated to study and understand their immediate surroundings and that they were quite capable of making intelligent qualitative assessments of them.

For the future Art and the Built Environment project, however, the most important element on Frontdoor was that Eileen Adams was the assistant head of art at Pimlico. She planned the studies, worked with the architects and began, systematically, to record what the children did. When the Art Committee of the Schools Council wanted to launch a project that would encourage a direct 'feeling' response to architecture and lead to the growth of critical awareness, she already had a great deal of relevant experience. When the new project was established at the Town and Country Planning Association under Colin Ward's direction she became the field officer. From 1976 to 1980 they worked with a number of trial schools in order to develop a range of methods that would enable teachers and children to study together. These were drawn from a wide range of sources but experience showed that they worked best when they could be linked, at least in the first place, with approaches already familiar in art teaching.

Just when this work was bearing fruit and quite a large number of schools wanted to be involved, the project looked like coming to an end. Colin Ward was retiring from the TCPA and the work could not continue there. After a good deal of hard bargaining, we were able to obtain the funds for a two-year extension to be based at the Royal College of Art. Eileen Adams became the director of the project.

The Schools Council saw the two-year extension as being for dissemination. We have seen it rather differently. Our aim has been to set up a network of local curriculum development groups in which, once again, architects and planners would join with teachers in affecting the work done in schools. Certainly we have 'disseminated' the project's store of knowledge and experience to the groups but we have also, and more importantly, invited them to take part in experiments to extend, refine and analyse the body of shared experience which we now have. Our 'enquiry' has been based in and made possible by the existence of the groups: their willingness to experiment and report on their experiences has been the research medium.

In September 1981, when we started this phase of the project, there were three of these working parties in existence. There are now 36 involving over 400 schools. Now that Schools Council funding is ending we believe that they have achieved sufficient reputation and support to continue with local authority and other backing.

I will now ask Eileen Adams to present her paper.

My particular focus is work derived from the Art and the Built Environment Project and the people who have been responsible for it. First, I would like us to consider the experience of promoting this area of curriculum development; and then to look in greater depth at the ideas and type of work that have been generated.

Promoting curriculum development

During the first three years of the Project, Colin Ward and I worked with art teachers in ten trials schools. I think it would be fair to say perhaps that from some schools we learnt things we hadn't known before; others confirmed what we already knew; and a few others perhaps came along for the ride. I now understand that this is a usual spread for trial schools in Schools Council projects. It would also be fair to say that the full range of ABE work was not covered, and in many cases not even attempted. There was of course much evidence of artwork based on environmental reference, but art teachers did not need a Schools Council project to tell them how to deal with that. There were some attempts at critical appraisal, but these were tentative and uncertain. There was little evidence of design activity.

Following the work in the trial schools, I embarked on an intensive programme of in-service work, and it soon became apparent that the courses which involved architects and planners were of particular value to teachers, offering them access to ideas and ways of thinking they had not previously encountered. In a number of cases, a working contract was established between architects and planners and teachers in schools, and subsequent meetings or courses arranged to report on the work. These were the beginnings of the Working Parties. Of course, parallel to this there were moves in other areas of general education to involve environmental professionals in work in schools and a growing interest in this from the professional bodies concerned with environmental design. The current phase of the Project has capitalised on this, and sought to introduce into schools experience and expertise that is not readily accessible in other ways. Its interest has been to promote a working partnership between teachers, architects and planners to influence what is taught in schools.

An important aspect of this co-operation is that normally the two groups involved tend to work in isolation. Teachers in the classroom still tend to work as individuals, and do not necesarily have direct access to ideas and practices other than their own. Similarly, although architects and planners may operate as members of design teams, they may have little working contact with the community and their everyday concerns about the environment. The establishment of a working partnership between the two groups has suggested ideas and ways of working not previously evident in schools and has enabled non-teachers to make a particular contribution to general education not possible in any other way.

In the ABE Project, we have tried to find different words that mean the same as 'environment' because it was being over-used or was clumsy, awkward or difficult. Similarly, I am continually trying to find words to describe and explain Working Parties – this phenomenon of groups from different professional backgrounds working together to influence what is taught in schools. It is necessary to search for different words, for not only do the groups differ greatly, but people perceive them differently. Even the label 'Working Party' poses problems. For some it suggests a group of people – all talk and no action, or more politely, an advisory committee; for others a hierarchical and tightly structured group directing operations; for still others, an elite 'in'-crowd capable of obscuring and jargonising the most simple ideas.

But the Working Parties involved in the ABE Project are none of these. We have tried to encourage only workers in Working Parties – people willing to experiment in schools with study activities designed to promote the aesthetic and design aspects of environmental study. These have included primary and secondary school teachers, architects and planners. In some groups, colleagues from higher education are also involved, and in a few cases, other environmental agencies, such as local amenity societies. Many of the groups are loosely structured, indeed one might go as far as saying hardly organised, while others provide strong encouragement and support for their members. Their

commitment is to try out ways of working and to report on the results of their work, to make it accessible so that others might learn from their experience.

The Working Parties phase of the ABE Project has been in operation for only two years. During that time, I have been pressured by the Schools Council to provide them with facts and figures about the groups – the numbers of schools involved, names of local authorities which support the work, details of finance, composition of groups, numbers of schools and so on. I have resisted this pressure to some degree, as I felt as if I was expected to pull up the tender young plant every few weeks to check on its growth.

I am not sure whether the Council understands the tentative, exploratory and, in some cases, transitory nature of the Working Parties. You will find that the number of groups mentioned in Project literature varies, depending on when the particular piece was written; this reflects the fluid nature of many groups, emerging, disappearing and reappearing, depending on the interest and stamina of the people involved. Similarly, groups themselves go through various stages in their development, with periods of innovation and consolidation, excitement and frustration.

We have been aware however of the need to evaluate the Working Parties' experience. It is evident that committed and gifted teachers are capable of innovatory work, but these will remain as individual and isolated examples unless there is a way to make the experience accessible, comprehensible and more generally available. This requires careful evaluation to determine what has been worthwhile in terms of both learning and teaching and to consider how others might benefit from knowing about it. The Project's view is that self-evaluation is of prime importance, and that a positive and critical stance about one's work is a necessary requirement. In the context of ABE work, criticism is seen as shared evaluation, whether that be in relation to townscape or work in schools, and the Working Party can fulfil this important critical function, encouraging members to reflect on their experience, to learn from it and to share it with others so that they too might learn.

The Project believes it is important to consider evaluation not so much in terms of 'what was' as 'what might be'. The important thing in curriculum development is not so much the success or failure of a particular experience, but what we can learn from it for future action. A major function of the ABE Summer School and exhibition held in July was to articulate what we have learnt from our experience over the last two years in order to promote new directions, in terms of both immediate initiatives and long-term planning.

Another element in this evaluation exercise is the study of seven groups which I am carrying out in order to report to the Schools Council Programme 2, concerned with 'helping teachers to become more effective'. I started this study in the Autumn Term last year, but have had to interrupt it because of preparing publications and the Summer School. However, I will resume my interview programme at the beginning of next term, and hope to complete the study by Easter.

I have selected seven Working Parties which represent a variety of groups in terms of membership, organisation, activities and work in schools. It would not be proper to reveal details of my study at this stage, though it is possible to draw on the study to make some general points about the experience of teachers, architects and planners working together in curriculum development groups.

I think at this stage I can say that the Project welcomes the challenge of such inter-professional co-operation, and is very aware of the benefits it brings as far as opening up an unfamiliar curriculum area is concerned. There are dangers of course. In some instances, architects and planners have been so successful in the classroom that teachers have tended to become more passive and have been happy to let others do their work for them. I doubt that the intention was ever for architects and planners to take over the teacher's role, but it is certainly not clear at the moment what the range of working relationships might be. Perhaps this is a point which will be considered in the discussion groups tomorrow.

Another important role is that of the co-ordinator. As well as organisation, it needs to be inspirational. The Project looks towards local authority advisers – and art advisers in particular – to provide the necessary leadership to promote the future development of ABE work. As far as the team is concerned, we have answered our brief: to identify appropriate study methods to develop ABE work in schools and to help establish a national network of local curriculum development groups to implement this.

It is perhaps appropriate here to recognise the value of national initiatives in curriculum development and to look at the role of a Project Team in relation to local groups. We have stressed the importance of co-operation between people from different professional backgrounds in this area of curriculum development and recognised the value of a network of groups generating ideas and experience, which provides a medium for innovation and consolidation.

However, we are well aware that a network is not just a list of addresses. It can only function if communication is based on personal contact and a shared programme of work. The need is for a strong personal commitment supported by an understanding that it is possible to make an individual contribution that will be valued. This must be the essential concern of the Project Team whose role is to interpret and give public recognition to these local efforts. It is now up to local

authorities to capitalise on their investment of money and their employees' time and effort by ensuring ABE finds a permanent place in schools.

What has been significant is that the Working Parties have demonstrated that it is possible for teachers and other colleagues interested in general education to work together to tackle the challenging question of what should be taught in schools. Their efforts suggest as a model of the curriculum one of continual evolution, capable of adapting to new needs and conditions in society.

The nature of the work

I hope I have given some idea of the way in which we have approached the promotion of curriculum development. I would like now to turn to the kinds of study activities that have been developed as a result of co-operation between the Working Parties and the Project Team.

In ABE work, the concern is not so much with a body of knowledge to be remembered, but of skills to be learned and capacities to be developed, of attitudes to be formed which will encourage a positive and creative stance in relation to participation in design and decision making. This is as true of the Working Party experience as it is of work in schools. Curriculum development is more to do with attitudes – those of pupils, teachers, parents and society in general – than it is to do with guidelines, kits, packs and learning resources. Our aims have been:

1   to enlarge students' environmental perception and enable them to develop a feel for the built environment
2   to enhance their capacity for discrimination and their competence in critical appraisal
3   evolve generally acceptable techniques and materials for achieving these aims and disseminate these in a form suitable for teacher training
4   develop a nationwide network of Working Parties, involving teachers, architects and planners in curriculum development.

Remembering that we are dealing with an *art* based study of aesthetics and design aspects of the built environment, it seems useful first of all to clarify three rather different approaches:

1   using the environment as a basis for art and design activity
2   using art and design activity as a way of understanding the environment
3   helping people to be involved in making decisions about the environment.

In terms of children's work, we can look at the range of different possibilities for learning experiences that these suggest.

The first we are all familiar with – the response of the artist: using the environment as a rich source of experience, stimulus and ideas as a basis for art work. The production of an art work enables us to reflect on the sensations, feelings and ideas derived from environmental experience and to come to terms with them, to understand that experience more fully and to use it as a basis for further learning.

The second theme – using art and design activity as a way of understanding the environment – emphasises the need to devise study methods which focus on the aesthetic and design aspects of environmental experience. Art, like any other subject discipline, offers a particular framework for study, a means of understanding, a way of knowing. In the work I will present, this has meant an emphasis on direct sensory experience, a recognition of the value of subjective, emotional response, a concern for the development of discriminatory and critical skills and the ability to make informed value judgements. The concern has been to bring the attitudes and values familiar in art and design education into the realm of environmental un-derstanding.

The third theme – helping people to be involved in making decisions about the environment – obliges us to think about our wider role as educators. In British schools, many children ask 'what is art for?' In this context, I suggest that our long-term aim might be to encourage and prepare people to take a more creative and participatory stance in shaping their environment in the future.

Expressions of creativity are to be found not only in the reproduction of paintings and sculpture, in visual, literary or other expressive art forms, but in how we shape our surroundings, how we operate, how we relate to the world in which we live.

The art teacher has perhaps been over-concerned with the development of production skills, the manipulation of expressive media. In art-based environmental work, the concern is also with experimental skills, with perceptual, discriminatory, analytical and critical skills as well of course as communicatory skills.

The teacher's responsibility is far greater than teaching children how to paint or pot or print. It is to extend their capacities for feeling and thinking and taking action.

As Ken Baynes explained in his introduction, Art and the Built Environment has been a six-year curriculum development project involving many pupils, teachers, architects and planners in action research, concerned with extending the boundaries of art in general education. It has been an area where art, design and environmental education interact, bringing a consideration of the attitudes and values of art education to environmental design. It can be viewed as a contribution of the art teacher to the general development of the design dimension of the school curriculum.

Analysis and synthesis, the recto and verso of design

Herman Neuckermans
K.U. Leuven – Afdeling Architektuur, Belgium

Traditional architectural design education is organised so as to confront students with problems of architectural design, arranged as a series of projects growing in complexity and differing according to approach, theme, context (real or fictitious) and technology.

However one can wonder if architectural design education cannot be approached in a different way, namely by acting upon the mental capabilities one expects a designer to have and by influencing the mentality with which a designer tackles any design problem.

Based upon the conviction that the poverty of architecture lies in its banality, we try to introduce a multi-faceted way of designing, in which a design is not the result of the addition of mono-functional solutions, but in which every part, as well as the whole, is built up in a pluri-functional way. The philosophy underlying this approach is that the more the solution induces stimuli, the less banal it will be; and the more it will leave traces in the mind, the more it becomes meaningful.

To reach this multi-valence in architecture and in its parts, we analyse thoroughly one specific building element, IC windows.

Nearly every architectural school has its own approach to the teaching of design: this very fact is remarkable enough and should give rise to thought.

However, there is more.

A curriculum for architectural design does not exist in isolation; it has to be based upon theoretical insights. A background from which design decisions can be taken has to be generated.

Such a theoretical insight into the purpose of building is the object of architectural theory: this encompasses the study of the meaning, for man and society, of architecture (the building and the built environment) and the transformations induced by architecture.

Too often architectural design methodology is considered as an autonomous field, detached from the subject of concern, ignoring its strong links with history and culture and therefore the learning of architectural background. This point of view finds its configuration in the definition of design as a creative act by pre-eminence. Indeed F. Barron[1] defines creativity as 'the easy recombination of ideas in the preconscious'. D. Mackinnon[2] says: 'From an associationistic viewpoint creativity is putting the elements of one's experiences into new combinations....' In other words there is a need for both previous experience, ideas, content and for the mental capability to recombine. Education should act on both.

The architectural theory provides the insights governing the designer's acts; this theory like many human sciences has as yet the status of 'paralogie', as argued by Lyotard.[3] Hereby he is referring to the fact that there is no longer a single truth, one single 'grand récit' as legitimation, but several (smaller) stories co-existing.

Rather as in the field of philosophy where a shift has occurred from a modern conception of science (Descartes, Popper, ...) to 'La condition postmoderne' under the influence of Kuhn, Feyerabend, Lakatos, Habermas *et al*, similarly a parallel evolution can be observed within architectural theory from Modernism to Post-Modernism, denying the existence of universal values and truths.[4] Given this situation, which should not be seen as a status of inferiority, the human sciences and *a fortiori* architectural theory cannot formulate normative rules.

Anyhow, any designer designs from an insight; insight and design stick together as do the recto and verso of a sheet of paper.

Considering this pluralism in thought and architecture, it does not seem very appropriate to argue for one specific way of shaping architecture. We therefore advocate an architectural quality, which transcends the discussion of architectural morphology. We argue for a quality which consists in making an architecture rich in felt experiences, an architecture dense with sensorial stimuli, rich in referential elements for plural use, an architecture which, through interpretation and use, becomes loaded with a multiplicity of meanings.

Often a design is treated as a mere addition of mono-functionally solved parts, due to the decomposition of the design problems into pieces (as is frequent in design methods). CIAM[5] once took apart the whole city in housing, working, recreation and circulation pieces; we know the result by now: a world taken apart, cities like trees.[6]

Still today many architects tackle their design problems with the same meagre mentality: one element serves one function. Likewise in education everything is split up: eg a construction technology course deals with construction-elements as if they exist without shape and meaning. The way one analyses and interprets the world conditions the way in which one acts, designs and comes to synthesis in the same world: analysis and synthesis coupled to each other and yet differing like the recto and the verso of design. In this way of looking at architecture we wish to intervene by highlighting the potentialities of an architecture of pluri-interpretations.

Such an architecture is plurifunctional in all its parts, stimulating several uses, fascinating in a multiplicity of ways. The richer the experience, the more it is worth experiencing. Let us take a few (somewhat simplified) examples:

A tourist in the Mediterranean ventures under water to discover a new world there; before he saw it, he was unaware that his Mediterranean experience would have been incomplete without it.

The one who looks at a non-figurative painting as a complete layman will probably only half understand it; the one however who is experienced in this kind of painting will probably understand and enjoy it much more.

This reasoning applies *mutatis mutandis* to architecture: 'apprendre à voir l'architecture'[7] should be taught from the primary school onwards, because architecture is a phenomenon with which all people are inevitably confronted.

Multiplicity of meaning is strongly linked with multiplicity of use.

If a designer wishes to stimulate a response, he will have to act on the factors that influence this activation; the 'collative' factors, so named by Berlyne, include 'complexity', 'novelty', 'incongruity', 'surprise'.[8] Later on Wohlwill started talking abut 'structural complexity' and 'diversity' rather than 'complexity', and also added 'ambiguity' to the set of collative factors.[9]

This terminology does not solely belong to the psychologist's jargon. Many authors have used these concepts, especially 'complexity' and 'ambiguity', in writings on architecture.[10] Eco highlights the importance of ambiguity as a stimulus for sensorial activation: indeed architecture can be seen as a means of communication, as carrying a message that can provoke an aesthetic[11] response: 'le message assume une fonction esthétique lorsqu'il est structuré d'une manière ambigue et auto-reflecsive, c'est à dire lorsqu'il entend attirer l'attention du destinataire sur sa forme avant tout'.[12]

Jencks talks about multivalence.[13] Frampton uses plurifunctionality in a somewhat different way: he advocates buildings or structures that can be used for several functions.[14] Herzberger's 'Centraal Beheer' in Apeldoorn (the Netherlands) can be seen as an example of this: though it has been designed as an office building it can easily be used as a school.

In this paper we advocate an architecture of plurifunctionality (not in its narrow, utilitarian meaning) in all its parts: an architecture composed of elements in which simultaneously several functions (uses) are interwoven, analogous to the way a text bears a multiplicity of meanings.[15] Barthes writes: 'Interpreter un texte, ce n'est pas lui donner un sens (plus ou moins fondé, plus ou moins libre); c'est au contraire apprécier de quel pluriel il est fait'.[16]

Architecture that wants to fascinate, to stimulate, should induce a multiplicity of intepretations: this presupposes design has a mentality of plurifunctionality: seeing many aspects and multiple

facets and subsequently introducing deliberate but not haphazard potentialities into the design product. In some cases this can result in an extremely sober, minimal, architecture. Indeed a picture does not need to be completely 'filled' in order to mean quite a lot.

A sober architecture, rich in potentialities, can however not exist without a rich insight.

As an illustration of this 'multiple' approach to architecture, let us take the example of the window,[17] because it is a very good example of what was stated above: there are plenty of books which deal with the technological aspects of windows and their quantifiable aspects; taken together they result in a distorted or biased picture of this guiding element.[18] Very little is written about its softer aspects, those which make the window part of an architectural whole. What we intend to do is to paint a rich image of windows, a multi-faceted image; we give a 'thick description' of windows, to use Geertz' words.[19]

The window as a transition

As a part of the outer wall the window regulates the transition from the inside to the outside, but does so in a very special way: the window-pane is both separation and link. Its meaning vibrates between two poles, depending on the observer's intention and depending on the differing light intensities in- and outside: the glass has a 'δυναμισ' according to J. Claes.[20]

Figure 1.
The window-pane acts as both separation and link between the inside and the outside.

Like all objects windows also determine the space around them: a space in front and behind the pane, a zone inside and a zone outside determined by more than climatic factors only. The window settles privacy: it is able to regulate in a very subtle and versatile way the inward and outward view: this is possible by way of the design of the window *stricto sensu,* and by way of the purposeful organisation of the space in front of and the space behind the window.

It is remarkable to note how inventive and subtle people have been in structuring this transition between in and outside using all kinds of devices conditioned by culture and religion. We think of eg: lattices, meshings, folding blinds, sliding panes, venetian blinds, louvres, persiennes, sunscreens, overhangs, windowbays, and the manifold forms derived from window design eg: balcony, loggia, alcove....[21]

The articulation of the transition between the inner and outer (through all kinds of patterns of voids and solids, through the interposition of screens, in-between spaces, barriers, points of control ...) reflects the mental transition between the private and the public domain, and is fundamental in man's behaviour.

When this transition neglects the cosmology of the inhabitant, conflicts arise, expressed in for example vandalism, barricading windows, hostility towards unwanted intruders in a domain that is officially public but considered by the inhabitants as private or semi-private.[22]

Only a close analysis of human behaviour by means of suitable anthropological categories, in relation to the way in which transition is organised, can give insight to such a complex phenomenon – and this complexity must be the basis for designing. A window is not only a link regulating the mental transition between in-and outside, but it is also the separation between the inner and outer climate. Often the window is the weakest link in this climatological transition: thermal and acoustic insulation have become particularly important as a consequence of rising comfort-demands, the energy crisis and urbanisation. These aspects can however easily be solved with a plurifunctional approach, eg in a situation of heavy sound exposure, the windows can be doubled with a wide space in between, which can be converted into a little botanical garden, a greenhouse or wintergarden, or as a sitting alcove: the inner-window can then be left open or can be closed according to the weather conditions.

The window as an element of the interior space

The space inside, near to the window, is a particular place: the natural light, the contact with the outside, with nature, with life, with moving people and objects, makes this place for a lot of people a favourite spot, for children and elderly people the window as a place to sit seems to be very important.

Figure 2.
The space inside, by the window, is a favourite place for many people.

The window is often a place for plants: plants grow with the changing light which close to the windows follows the natural movement of sun and clouds, the day and night and seasons.

In our cultural context we see more and more screens of green plants in the window space, possibly as a substitute for the green which is often missing from the immediate housing environment. The window determines the 'framing' of the environment (it is not casual that in computer graphics 'windowing' is used to frame a picture on the CRT), provides, hides or masks views.

Horizontal and vertical windows provide substantially differing visual information as well as experience value: horizontal windows have a horizontal stratification of the outlook as a consequence; vertical windows induce a movement parallax: a kind of 'motion in between the pictures' as in film. With a horizontal window the picture is more static at least with regard to the observer's movement; through the vertical window we may see a part of the sky, the remote and the immediate environment. The vertical window, associated with high interiors, has a connotation of richness, with high incoming light, deep-reaching and pleasantly surprising. Glare and hard contrasts between glass panes or between the window and the adjoining wall parts can be avoided by bevelling the inside corners and providing windows in at least two walls of the same space. The window gives an orientation to the interior: eg with the design of a bay window new possibilities for sunlighting, views and screening come about. The interior window links inner spaces; in a special way it gives free unexpected views; it keeps spatial visual relation and eliminates at one go possible sound hindrance.

The window as façade design element

The way in which building and inhabitants are involved with the environment can be read in the openings of the outer wall: number, form, size, detailing, material, framing, division, articulation, scale, proportion, rhythm, colour, and last but not least the way in which the inhabitant personalises his windows determine the character of the façade.

Much more could be said about all these aspects, but we would go beyond the scope of this paper. We confine ourselves here to one aspect, which has often been badly treated: repetition of identical elements. It can make a façade fascinating on condition that the whole gets a new identity, an added value in comparison to the separate elements (eg Crescent Gardens, London); if not, repetition induces monotony.

The one who designs with this complexity in mind, cannot make a window that merely fills an opening in a wall. The one who 'reads' an environment in this way, will 'write' the environment in similarly.

The one who thus analyses, will so design and synthesise – analysis and synthesis: the recto and verso of a design.

This text advocates a quality of architecture: multiplicity of meaning. For that purpose the window has been chosen as an example; it has the advantage of being at the same time limited and concrete, and yet still broad enough to avoid a simplification of the exposé on architecture to a technical discussion or to a mechanistic analysis of design.

References

1 Barron, F. 'Creativity', in *Encyclopedia Brittanica*, vol 6, p 711–712.
2 Mackinnon, D. 'Creativity: a multi-faceted phenomenon' in: Roslansky, J.D. e.a. (Ed.) *Creativity: a discussion at the Nobel conference, 1970*, North-Holland, Amsterdam, 1970, p 17–33.
3 Lyotard, J.F. *La condition postmoderne*, Minuit, Paris, 1979, p 63.
4 Heynen, H. *Het postmodernisme in de architectuur en in de architectuur theorie – Een wetenschapsfilosofische benadering*, Thesis, Afdeling Architectuur – KU Leuven (B), 1981.
5 CIAM is the acronym for the Congrès Internationaux d'Architecture Moderne.
6 Alexander, C. 'A city is not a tree' in *Design*, no 206, Feb 1966, p 46–55.
7 Levi, B. Apprendre à voir l'architecture, Minuit, Paris, 1959.
8 Berlyne, D. *Conflict, arousal and curiosity*, McGraw-Hill, New York, 1960.
9 Wohlwill, J. 'Environmental aesthetics: the environment as a source of conflict' in: Altman, I. & Wohlwill, J. *Human Behavior and environment*, Plenum Press, New York, 1976.
10 Rappoport, A. & Cantor, R. 'Complexity and Ambiguity', in *Journal of American Institute of Planners*, July 1967, p 210–221.
11 'Aesthetic' in its original Greek meaning (aithesis).
12 ECO, U. *La structure absente: Introduction à la recherche sémiotique*, Mercure de France, Paris, 1972.
13 Jencks, C. *Modern Movements in Architecture*, Penguin, Harmondsworth, 1973.
14 Frampton, K. 'Reflection on the Opposition of Architecture and Building', p 112 in Gowan, J. (ed.) *A Continuing Experiment*, AA Press, London, 1975, p 107–113.
15 Loeckx, A. *Model en Metafoor – bijdragen tot een semantisch-praxeologische benadering van bouwen en wonen* (3 vols), PhD thesis, Afedling Architektuur, KU Leuven (B), 1982.
16 Barthes, R. S/Z, Seuil, Paris, 1970.
17 We are discussing windows here in the context of housing. This survey could gain a lot by a cross-cultural, as well as by a historical study of windows.
18 See the following:
Beckett, H. & Godfrey, J. *Windows – performance, design and installation*, Crosby Lockwood Staples, London, 1974.
De Feyter, P. *Architecturale aspecten van vensters* (2 vols.) Thesis afdeling architectuur, KU Leuven, (B), 1980; also *Het Raam*, 1981.
Duell, J., 'Windows part 1' *AJ*, 6 June 79, p 1179–1188.
Duell, J., 'Windows part 2' *AJ*, 4 July 79, p 31–53.
Nueckermans, H. & Simon, J. *Functionele studie van de woning*, CHC, Brussels, 1975, and *Het raam* in *Bouwawereld*, nr. 7, (27 March), 1981, 153 p (special issue).
19 Geertz, C. 'The interpretation of cultures' in *Selected essays*, Hutchinson, London, 1975, pp 3–30.
20 Claes, J. *De dingen en hun ruimte,* Nederlandse Boekhandel, Antwerpen 1970.
21 Alexander, C. *A pattern language,* Oxford University Press, New York, 1977, pattern numbers: 127, 128, 135, 159, 161, 163–168, 179, 180, 192, 194, 197, 202, 221, 231, 238, 239, 240.
22 Loeckx, A. *op cit*, Deel 3.
23 Markus, T. 'The function of windows – a reappraisal', p 103 in *Building Science*, vol 2 no 2, 1967, pp 97–121.

Cultural-historical awareness: an aspect in the education of industrial designers

Dietmar Palloks
Kunsthochschule Berlin, GDR

Training of industrial designers is connected with national-economic conditions and objectives and with the requirements and cultural needs of the people. Essential contents of teaching are:

— mediation and training of artistic-designing and its scientific foundations
— developing method
— developing responsibility for society and a deep humanist objective

Industrial design influences and 'structures' the relationship between the consumer/user and the product. Thus products reflect a way of life within a concrete socio-cultural environment.

The relationship between the user and the product becomes more comprehensible if the designer, among other things, understands his present design activities as part of a cultural process, and if he, by historical analogy, obtains insights for the future. This aspect of a design approach, which I should like to define as cultural-historic consciousness, will gain in importance in the future. Functionally emphasised designed products with relative longevity are a consequence of this attitude.

I have given my short observations the title: 'Cultural-Historical Awareness – an Aspect in the Education of Industrial Designers.'

Two introductory points:

1 I do not propose to give you a comprehensive survey of design education in the German Democratic Republic but have limited myself to a few particular aspects of design education at the Art College in Berlin.
2 A cultural-historical awareness is not an official aim of the course. Yet its foundations must be laid, at the very latest, at college level and a relevant approach aroused and developed in the students.

If design education is not to fall short of its aim, it must be so devised that both teacher and student think ahead and, in keeping with the aims of society, plan new user-product relationships[1] and take part in the sketching of the 'face of things to come.' The teaching must impart principles that will be valid for a long time into the future. We try to provide a training that comes near to the practice – practice, however, is not a synonym for the present; practice is the probable tomorrow, too.

During the course a broad and solid subject-related basis should evolve. In essence, this basis must be capable of broadening out and provide for a continual growth in knowledge. A solid foundation can be basically achieved by:

1 the imparting and the cultivating of a basic artistic-designing, technically-constructive, scientific understanding,
2 the developing of the ability to solve problems,
3 the developing and strengthening of an attitude, which is marked by a social sense of responsibility and a deep humanity.

At the beginning of their studies, the students concentrate on drawing, colour, sculpture, letter-formation and other basic areas in the visual arts. These courses are taken in common by the students from a variety of departments, such as Architecture, Graphics, Fashion, Painting, Sculpture and Stage Design to name but a few. The students come to the college from very varying art-educational backgrounds. The general art foundation course in the first year evens out these differences to some extent. The students are prepared for their future tasks in their special subject.

In the subject-orientated foundation courses[2] close adherence to nature and natural forms are relinquished as far as is possible. At this stage students concentrate on the aesthetic quality of their work. An aesthetic order develops with a high structural complexity but with few complications. In this way the following qualities are developed:

— a sensitivity for form, colour and surface qualities[3]
— a sense of proportion
— the ability to discern according to visual-aesthetic quality
— manual capabilities.

The first designs worked at are simple, technical products; later they become more complex. I do not want to go into questions of design methods – too much has already been said and written about the subject.

An important moment in the course is the practical co-operation with consumer groups and manufacturers. This can have the following results:

— Co-operation with consumers. The real, actual needs can be quickly assessed and the future use-value determined with greater certainty. In this way products can be made that have been developed for a concrete circle of customers, possibly for urgent and immediate use, but which have not had to be manufactured first.
— Didactically, a totally different situation arises from the co-operation with factories, which determine the materials and techniques used themselves and are looking for ideas for products that can be manufactured and which can contribute to the satisfaction of consumer needs as far as they can be determined in detail.
— The most common form of practical work during the course is the close co-operation with industry in the development of products. Engineers,

technologists, economists and designers work together on one task. Students learn a lot from such work. They recognise their place in the course of development and learn, step by step, the discipline that is a part of co-operation in the production process. They recognise their achievements as an integral part of the development of a product and learn to feel responsibility for their unique and vital activity: creating aesthetic form.[4]

The socially orientated, humanist position of the designer, as the representative of consumer interests, necessitates the practical application of design-historical knowledge. And by that I do not mean the design-historical education taken from the pattern of early bourgeois art appreciation.

The question concerning the satisfaction of consumer needs in former times must be answered. The visual appearance alone of old products gives us no information as to how these needs were satisfied. The museums are full of old objects. But the exhibits often do no more than close the mind of an observer, particularly when the consumer objects are put on display as works of art – they stiffen into antiquated decoration.

The designer is interested in detailed examination of the structure of the social class in which the product tended to be used, of the way of life of the consumer,[5] the way in which the objects were used and how they were made and produced etc. Only the results of such research can give any information about a product and its significance for the user: With these insights, practising designers are able to acquire a true understanding of the user-product relationship. They see their present design activities as a part of a cultural process, embedded between past and future and by drawing conclusions from past and present situations, gain knowledge for the future. I would like to call this approach to design the cultural-historical awareness. It will gain significance in the future in connection with the question: 'What and how much do people really need?'

New scientific technical knowledge, new technologies and people's growing and developing needs will, on the one hand, open up new opportunities for use value, but on the other hand, the shortage of raw materials and resources in the world, the polluting of the environment through industry and in other ways,[6] will make new solutions urgently necessary. The designer must be prepared to solve the problems of the future and to be able to react flexibly to changing situations. The graduates, who will leave college this year as qualified designers, will in the year 2000 only have about half their professional lives behind them ....

In our course we try to teach the cultural-historical side to functional objects through practical work in a

museum.[7] The aim of such research is not the collecting of facts and data. It is rather a training that gains cultural-historical insights for the students, which in turn determine certain ways of looking at things and behaviour. The museum in which we are allowed to work is primarily concerned with the work of the people from a rural area. The functional objects that were widespread in this area and to some extent are still typical today, are photographed, measured, sketched and verbally described by the students. Their origin and age, the technology and materials used in their production and the way in which they were used are determined. The way of life of the consumer or user and the social structure of the mainly village community are examined. To this end, old people from the area are questioned, craftsmen, who to some extent still know and are able to use the old technologies, are visited, and written sources, such as chronicles, are evaluated. Such inquiries result in a particular way of looking at things, in an attitude that leads to an understanding of the functional objects of former times. This way of looking at things encourages an understanding of cultural processes and historical connections. The inquiries are a practical contribution to and complement the lectures on design-history. They can act as a regulator on the overrating of stylish tendencies and demand respect from us for the achievements of past generations. Our quality measuring stick (by which I do not mean so much the quality of, for example, a surface refinement, as the quality of the user–product relationship) is influenced by them. They promote an awareness of tradition and raise the understanding for evolutionary processes in the development of production. Such inquiries change apparently non-historical relics of past times into speaking witnesses of their time, products with a history and surrounded by history. They become the acceptable 'relations' of today's product generations.

I hope that one consequence of such a way of looking at things will be the acknowledgement of the relative longevity of products and to design with a stress on function. I am sure that the longevity of functionally-designed products can provide a small contribution to the solving of the anticipated problems of the coming decade – most of the questions that concern us demand political solutions anyway.

References

1 Palloks, Dietmar, 'Schon wieder ein neuer Stuhl ...', in *Möbel und Wohnraum*, no 3, 1982.
2 Petroff-Bohne, Christa, 'Farbe', in *Form + Zweck* no 1, 1981, p 20.
3 Petroff-Bohne, Christa, 'Materialübungen, in *Form + Zweck*', no 6, 1981, p 16.
4 Hückler, Alfred, 'Das Unersetzbare an der Formgestaltung', in *Form + Zweck*, no 5, 1975, p 30.

5   Ausstellungskatalog '*Lebensgeschichten*', Centrum
    Industriekultur, Nürnberg, 1980.
6   Laptew, Iwan, *Planet ohne Zukunft*? Verlag Neues
    Leben, Berlin, 1976.
7   Palloks, Dietmar, 'Praktikum im Museum', in *Form +
    Zweck* no 1, 1981, p 24.